D1408811

PASTA
AND
RICE

WILTON HOUSE

Editor Angela Rahaniotis
Graphic Design Zapp
Photography Marc Bruneau
Food Preparation / Stylist Josée Robitaille
Assistant Stylist Marc Maula
Tableware courtesy of Ma Maison

Wilton House is an imprint of Joshua Morris Publishing Inc.,
221 Danbury Road, Wilton, CT 06897

10 9 8 7 6 5 4 3 2 1

ISBN 0-88705-850-7

PASTA
AND
RICE

If you are like most cooks, you are always on the lookout for interesting recipes that are easy to prepare, nutritious, and delicious.

In that case, this cookbook will quickly become a favorite. It is packed with easy-to-follow, full-color recipes based on two popular and economical ingredients – pasta and rice.

You will quickly discover that these foods lend themselves to far more than the old standbys of spaghetti with meat sauce or plain boiled rice. You'll find recipes for every occasion, from simple family meals to elegant dinners.

Best of all, pasta and rice are excellent sources of complex carbohydrates. The latest nutritional guidelines recommend that we should all be cutting down on fat and increasing our consumption of complex carbohydrates. And if you are watching your weight, this advice is especially important.

So get adventurous – and explore the many exciting ways pasta and rice can add variety and good nutrition to your menu.

Pasta

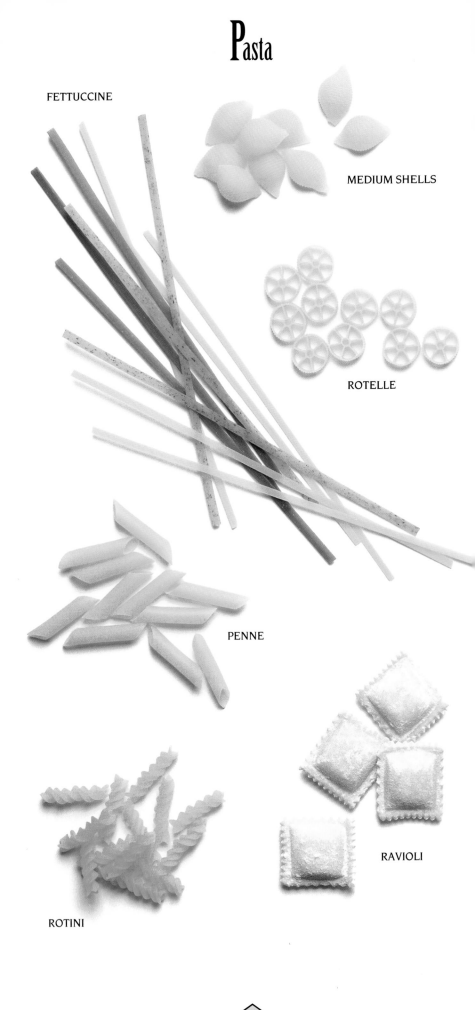

FETTUCCINE

MEDIUM SHELLS

ROTELLE

PENNE

RAVIOLI

ROTINI

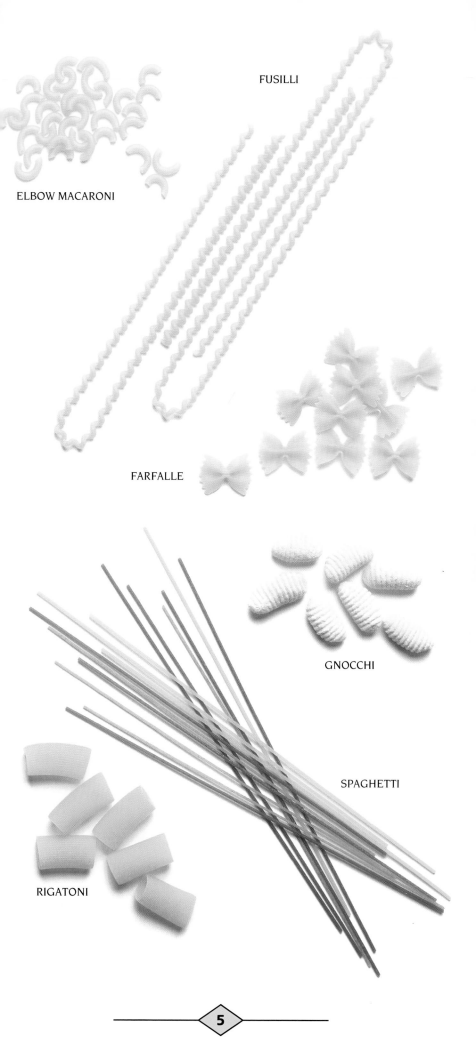

FUSILLI

ELBOW MACARONI

FARFALLE

GNOCCHI

SPAGHETTI

RIGATONI

LASAGNETTE

TORTELLINI

CAPELLI D'ANGELO
("ANGEL'S HAIR")

LINGUINE

EGG NOODLES

ZITI

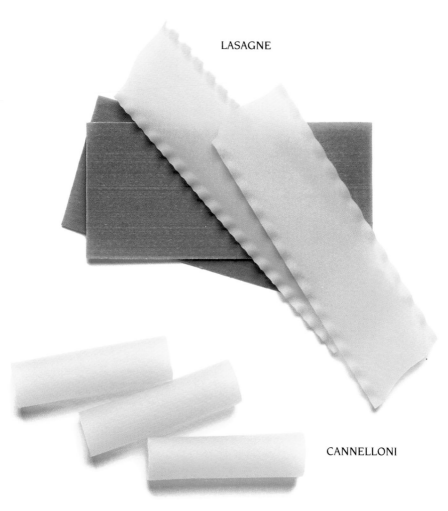

LASAGNE

CANNELLONI

Rice

ARBORIO RICE

BASMATI RICE

BROWN RICE

LONG GRAIN WHITE RICE

Pasta Dough

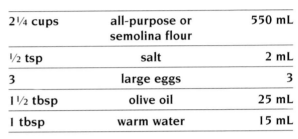

2¼ cups	all-purpose or semolina flour	550 mL
½ tsp	salt	2 mL
3	large eggs	3
1½ tbsp	olive oil	25 mL
1 tbsp	warm water	15 mL

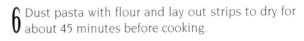

1 Place flour, salt, eggs, olive oil and water in large bowl.

2 Work dough with fingers to incorporate. Add more flour or water as needed. Dough should gather into a ball.

3 Turn out dough onto floured work surface. Knead dough 8 to 10 minutes, until smooth.

4 Shape dough into ball, dust with flour and place in bowl. Cover and let rest 1 hour at room temperature.

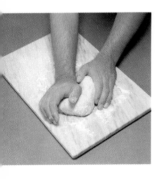

5 Cut dough into 4 pieces. Roll out each piece using a pasta machine and cut into strips.

6 Dust pasta with flour and lay out strips to dry for about 45 minutes before cooking.

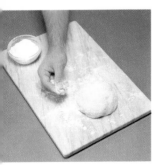

How to Cook Pasta

1 All pasta, whether fresh or dry, must be cooked in plenty of boiling salted water. Add a few drops of oil to the water to control foaming.

2 Only add pasta to the pot once the water has reached a full, rolling boil. Add pasta gradually, about ⅓ of the total amount at a time, to maintain the boil. As pieces soften slightly, stir to prevent sticking.

3 When water resumes a full boil, start timing the cooking process. Pasta is best served *al dente*, which means "to the tooth" in Italian. Cooked noodles should have a slight resistance and not be too soft. The best way to determine if the pasta is cooked, is to taste it.

4 When done, drain pasta well but do not rinse. Transfer pasta to heated platter or bowl, greased with olive oil or butter. Mix and use immediately.

Quick Gnocchi Dough
(4 to 6 servings)

6	large potatoes, boiled unpeeled	6
2	eggs, beaten	2
4 tbsp	melted butter	60 mL
1 cup	grated Parmesan cheese	250 mL
1 tsp	salt	5 mL
1¼ cups	all-purpose flour	300 mL
3 cups	Bolognese Meat Sauce (see p.88)	750 mL
1 cup	grated mozzarella cheese	250 mL
	freshly ground pepper	

1 Peel potatoes and force through food mill or potato ricer into bowl. Add eggs, butter, Parmesan cheese and salt. Mix together.

2 Add flour, little by little, mixing well between additions. Turn out dough onto floured work surface. If dough is too soft, add more flour. Knead dough until it becomes stiff.

3 Cut dough into 4 equal parts. Shape each part into a cylinder, about 1 in (2.5 cm) in diameter. Cut into pieces about ¾ in (2 cm) long.

4 Drop gnocchi into boiling salted water. Simmer 3 minutes over low heat. Gnocchi will rise to surface when cooked. Remove with slotted spoon and drain well.

5 Transfer gnocchi to buttered baking dish. Cover with hot meat sauce, season with pepper and top with cheese. Bake 20 minutes in oven, preheated at 375°F (180°C).

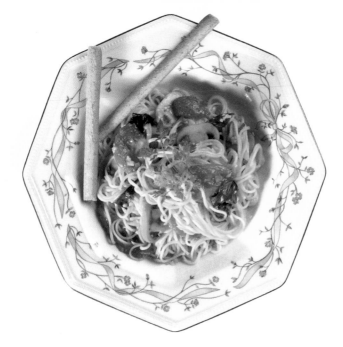

Capelli d'Angelo Nouvelle
(4 servings)

2	large tomatoes	2
2 tbsp	butter	30 mL
1	shallot, peeled and chopped	1
2	garlic cloves, peeled, crushed and chopped	2
12	large mushrooms, cleaned and sliced	12
15	fresh basil leaves	15
½ cup	dry white wine	125 mL
½ cup	chicken stock, heated	125 mL
1 lb	capelli d'angelo*, cooked al dente	450 g
1 cup	grated Parmesan cheese	250 mL
	salt and pepper	

1 Core tomatoes and cut into quarters. Remove seeds and slice each quarter into three. Set aside.

2 Heat butter in large sauté pan over medium heat. Add shallot, garlic and mushrooms; season well. Cook 2 minutes. Remove mushrooms from pan and set aside.

3 Add tomatoes and basil to pan; season and cook 2 minutes over medium heat. Pour in wine and increase heat to high; cook 2 minutes.

4 Return mushrooms to pan and pour in chicken stock. Mix, season and cook 1 minute over high heat.

5 Mix hot pasta with sauce in pan. Sprinkle in cheese, mix and simmer 2 minutes. Serve.

* This pasta is often referred to as "angel hair" pasta. The noodles are long and very delicate.

Rotelle Spinach Salad with Mustard Vinaigrette
(4 servings)

3	bunches fresh spinach	3
½ lb	rotelle, cooked al dente	225 g
4	green onions, cut in 1-in (2.5-cm) lengths	4
1	yellow bell pepper, thinly sliced	1
2	carrots, pared and grated	2
1	apple, cored, peeled and sliced	1
5	slices bacon, cooked crisp and chopped	5
⅓ cup	grated cheese of your choice	75 mL
1 tbsp	Dijon mustard	15 mL
3 tbsp	wine vinegar	45 mL
9 tbsp	olive oil	135 mL
	salt and pepper	
	juice of ½ lemon	

1 Remove stems from spinach. Wash leaves in plenty of cold water and spin dry.

2 Place spinach and pasta in large bowl. Add vegetables, apple, bacon and cheese.

3 Place salt, pepper and mustard in separate, smaller bowl. Add vinegar and whisk together. Add oil and whisk to incorporate.

4 Correct seasoning of vinaigrette and add lemon juice. Whisk and pour over salad ingredients. Mix well and serve.

Seafood Linguine
(4 servings)

2 tbsp	olive oil	30 mL
1	onion, peeled and finely chopped	1
2	garlic cloves, peeled, crushed and chopped	2
1/2 lb	large shrimp, peeled, deveined, and sliced in two	225 g
1/2 cup	dry white wine	125 mL
4	tomatoes, peeled, seeded and chopped	4
1 tbsp	chopped fresh parsley	15 mL
1/4 tsp	crushed chilies	1 mL
1/2 cup	pine nuts	125 mL
1 lb	linguine, cooked al dente	450 g
	salt and pepper	
	juice of 1/2 lemon	

1 Heat oil in frying pan over medium heat. Add onion and garlic; cook 3 minutes. Add shrimp and season well. Continue cooking 2 minutes.

2 Remove shrimp from pan and set aside.

3 Add wine, tomatoes, parsley, crushed chilies, salt and pepper to pan. Cook 8 minutes over medium heat.

4 Return shrimp to pan with tomatoes. Add pine nuts and lemon juice. Simmer 2 minutes.

5 Serve over hot pasta.

Fettuccine in Cream Sauce with Asparagus
(4 servings)

1 lb	fresh asparagus	450 g
¼ cup	heavy cream	50 mL
3	egg yolks	3
⅓ cup	melted butter	75 mL
½ cup	grated Parmesan cheese	125 mL
2	green onions, chopped	2
1 lb	fettuccine, cooked al dente	450 g
	salt and pepper	

1 Pare asparagus if necessary and trim stem ends. Cut stalks into 1-in (2.5-cm) pieces. Blanch pieces 3 minutes in boiling, salted water. Drain and place in bowl of cold water.

2 Mix cream and egg yolks together in bowl. Add three quarters of melted butter and mix well. Add cheese and season; mix again.

3 Heat remaining butter in frying pan over medium heat. Add drained asparagus and green onions. Cook 3 minutes.

4 Place hot pasta in heated stainless steel bowl. Add cream mixture, asparagus and green onions. Mix together well and correct seasoning. Serve.

Four-Cheese Macaroni
(4 servings)

I lb	macaroni, cooked al dente	450 g
¼ cup	diced mozzarella cheese	50 mL
¼ cup	diced Gruyère cheese	50 mL
¼ cup	grated Pecorino cheese	50 mL
¼ cup	melted butter	50 mL
¼ cup	cooking liquid from pasta	50 mL
¼ cup	grated Parmesan cheese	50 mL
	salt and freshly ground pepper	

Preheat oven to 400°F (200°C).

1 Place hot pasta in heated stainless steel bowl.

2 Add mozzarella, Gruyère and Pecorino cheeses; mix well. Season with salt and pepper.

3 Mix melted butter with cooking liquid from pasta. Pour over pasta, mix well and season with pepper. Transfer pasta to baking dish. Top with grated Parmesan cheese. Bake 6 to 8 minutes in oven.

Macaroni alla Caciocavallo
(4 servings)

¹/₃ cup	olive oil	75 mL
2	garlic cloves, peeled, crushed and chopped	2
1	chili pepper, seeded and chopped	1
1	onion, peeled and finely chopped	1
6 oz	prosciutto, finely chopped	175 g
6	tomatoes, peeled, seeded and chopped	6
1 lb	macaroni, cooked al dente	450 g
1 cup	grated Caciocavallo cheese	250 mL
	salt and pepper	

1 Heat oil in sauté pan over medium heat. Add garlic and chili pepper; cook 1 minute. Add onion and reduce heat to low; cook 3 minutes.

2 Add prosciutto and continue cooking 2 minutes. Stir in tomatoes, season well and cook 30 minutes over low heat.

3 Alternate layers of hot pasta, tomato sauce and cheese in baking dish. Repeat, finishing with layer of cheese. Broil in oven until cheese browns, then serve pasta at once.

Baked Macaroni and Cheese with Meat Sauce
(4 servings)

2 tbsp	olive oil	30 mL
1	onion, peeled and finely chopped	1
2	garlic cloves, peeled, crushed and chopped	2
¾ lb	lean ground beef	350 g
1 cup	dry red wine	250 mL
28 oz	can plum tomatoes, drained and chopped	796 mL
1 tbsp	chopped fresh parsley	15 mL
1 tbsp	chopped fresh basil	15 mL
¾ lb	macaroni, cooked al dente	350 g
⅔ cup	grated Parmesan cheese	150 mL
7	slices strong Provolone cheese	7
	salt and pepper	

Preheat oven to 350°F (180°C).

1 Heat oil in frying pan over medium heat. Add onion and garlic; mix and cook 4 minutes over medium heat.

2 Add ground beef and season well. Cook 4 minutes over medium heat. Pour in wine and continue cooking 4 minutes.

3 Add tomatoes and seasonings. Mix well, cover and cook 15 minutes over low heat.

4 Fill bottom of buttered baking dish with half of hot macaroni. Add half of meat sauce and sprinkle with Parmesan cheese. Repeat layers and top with slices of Provolone cheese.

5 Bake 20 minutes in oven.

Fettuccine with Smoked Salmon and Tomatoes
(4 servings)

2 tbsp	olive oil	30 mL
2	shallots, peeled and chopped	2
2	garlic cloves, peeled, crushed and chopped	2
½ cup	dry white wine	125 mL
2 tbsp	chopped fresh basil	30 mL
4	tomatoes, peeled, seeded and chopped	4
½ cup	heavy cream	125 mL
1 tbsp	butter	15 mL
1	yellow bell pepper, thinly sliced	1
3 oz	smoked salmon, cut in strips ½ in (1 cm) wide	90 g
1 lb	fettuccine, cooked al dente	450 g
	salt and pepper	
	grated Parmesan cheese	

1 Heat oil in sauté pan over medium heat. Add shallots and garlic; cook 2 minutes. Pour in wine and continue cooking 1 minute.

2 Add basil and tomatoes. Season well and continue cooking 8 minutes. Pour in cream, stir and cook 4 minutes.

3 Meanwhile, heat butter in saucepan over medium heat. Add yellow pepper and cook 3 minutes. Add smoked salmon and simmer 2 minutes over low heat.

4 Add hot pasta to tomato sauce in pan. Add yellow pepper and salmon. Toss, simmer 1 minute and serve with Parmesan cheese.

Seafood Fettuccine in Smoky Sauce
(4 servings)

1 lb	fettuccine, cooked al dente	450 g
3 tbsp	butter	45 mL
1 ⅓ cups	heavy cream	325 mL
3 oz	prosciutto, sliced in julienne	90 g
½ lb	fresh crabmeat	225 g
1 tbsp	chopped fresh chervil	15 mL
1 tbsp	chopped fresh parsley	15 mL
	salt and white pepper	
	cayenne pepper to taste	
	grated Pecorino Sardo cheese	

1 Place hot pasta in heated bowl and mix in butter. Cover and keep warm.

2 Cook cream 2 minutes in sauté pan over medium heat to thicken. Add prosciutto, crabmeat and herbs. Season well and simmer 2 minutes.

3 Toss in hot pasta. Season with cayenne pepper to taste. Simmer 2 minutes over low heat.

4 Grate Pecorino Sardo cheese over portions and serve.

Farfalle with Mushrooms and Bacon
(4 servings)

1 tbsp	butter	15 mL
2 oz	piece bacon, diced	60 g
3 tbsp	chopped shallots	45 mL
1	small red bell pepper, chopped	1
1 lb	fresh mushrooms, cleaned and halved	450 g
1/2 cup	dry white wine	125 mL
2 tbsp	coarsely chopped fresh basil	30 mL
1 1/4 cups	heavy cream	300 mL
1 lb	farfalle*, cooked al dente	450 g
	salt and pepper	
	pinch of paprika	
	grated Parmesan cheese	

1 Heat butter in large frying pan over medium heat. Add bacon and cook 4 minutes until well cooked. Remove bacon from pan and set aside.

2 Add shallots, red pepper and mushrooms to hot pan. Season well and cook 4 minutes over medium heat. Pour in wine and increase heat to high; cook 2 minutes. Remove vegetables from pan and set aside.

3 Return pan to stove over high heat. Add basil, cream and paprika; cook 4 minutes.

4 Season well and return bacon and vegetables to pan with sauce. Mix and add hot pasta. Toss and simmer 2 minutes.

5 Serve with Parmesan cheese.

* Farfalle is a bow-tie shaped pasta.

Fettuccine Jambalaya
(4 to 6 servings)

1 tbsp	olive oil	15 mL
6 oz	piece smoked ham, cubed	175 g
3	slices bacon, diced	3
1	onion, peeled and diced	1
28 oz	can tomatoes	796 mL
1	red chili pepper, seeded and chopped	1
2	bay leaves	2
4	sprigs thyme	4
4	sprigs parsley	4
10	fresh basil leaves	10
2	garlic cloves, unpeeled	2
1	celery stalk, cut in 2	1
½ tsp	cumin	2 mL
1 lb	fettuccine, cooked al dente	450 g
	salt and pepper	
	grated Parmesan cheese	

1 Heat oil in sauté pan over medium heat. Add ham, bacon and onion. Cook 5 minutes. Add tomatoes with juice and chili pepper; season well.

2 Place bay leaves, fresh herbs and garlic between pieces of celery; secure together with string. Add to sauce.

3 Stir in cumin and cook sauce 45 minutes over low heat. Do not cover.

4 Discard celery with herbs, add hot pasta to sauce and simmer 3 minutes. Serve with cheese.

Macaroni and Celeriac Salad
(4 servings)

I cup	grated peeled celeriac	250 mL
I	onion, peeled and chopped	I
I tbsp	chopped fresh basil	15 mL
I tbsp	chopped fresh parsley	15 mL
1/2 cup	plain yogurt	125 mL
1/2	celery stalk, diced	1/2
2	carrots, pared and grated	2
1/4 cup	mayonnaise	50 mL
2 tbsp	wine vinegar	30 mL
1/2 tsp	prepared mustard	2 mL
6 oz	macaroni, cooked al dente	175 g
	salt and pepper	
	juice of 1/2 lemon	
	lettuce leaves	

1 Blanch celeriac in salted, boiling water for 3 minutes. Drain well, cool and squeeze out any excess liquid. Set aside.

2 Place onion, basil, parsley and yogurt in bowl. Season well and mix together. Marinate I hour.

3 Add celeriac, celery and carrots to yogurt mixture. Mix and season, then stir in pasta.

4 In separate bowl, mix mayonnaise, vinegar and mustard together. Add to bowl containing vegetables and mix well.

5 Add lemon juice and correct seasoning. If more dressing is desired, add mayonnaise and vinegar to taste.

6 Serve on lettuce leaves.

Pasta Salad with Mixed Vegetables
(4 to 6 servings)

I	red bell pepper	I
I lb	fresh asparagus	450 g
I	small head broccoli	I
¼ cup	wine vinegar	50 mL
2	garlic cloves, peeled, crushed and chopped	2
2 tbsp	chopped fresh basil	30 mL
¾ cup	olive oil	175 mL
¼ cup	grated Parmesan cheese	50 mL
½ lb	fresh mushrooms, cleaned and sliced	225 g
½ cup	pitted black olives, sliced	125 mL
I lb	rotini or farfalle, cooked al dente	450 g
	salt and pepper	

1 Cut bell pepper in half and remove seeds. Oil skin and place cut-side-down on cookie sheet; broil 6 minutes in oven. Remove from oven and let cool. Peel off skin, slice pepper thinly and set aside.

2 Pare asparagus, if necessary, and trim stem ends. Cut stalks into 1-in (2.5-cm) pieces. Divide broccoli into florets. Blanch both vegetables in salted, boiling water. Set aside to drain well.

3 Place vinegar, garlic, basil, salt and pepper in mixing bowl. Whisk together. Add oil in thin stream while whisking to incorporate. Add cheese and whisk again.

4 Place bell pepper and blanched vegetables in large bowl. Add remaining ingredients, then pour in dressing.

5 Mix well, correct seasoning and serve.

Zesty Linguine
(4 servings)

3 tbsp	olive oil	45 mL
1 ½	red onions, peeled and thinly sliced	1 ½
2	garlic cloves, peeled, crushed and chopped	2
¾ lb	Italian sausages, sliced ¾ in (2 cm) thick	350 g
1 tbsp	chopped chili pepper	15 mL
12	fresh basil leaves, chopped	12
1 lb	linguine, cooked al dente	450 g
4 tbsp	grated Parmesan cheese	60 mL
	freshly ground pepper	

1 Heat oil in frying pan over medium heat. Add onions and cook 8 minutes over medium heat. Stir twice during cooking.

2 Add garlic, sausages, chili pepper and basil. Cook 3 to 4 minutes over medium heat. Season with pepper.

3 Add hot pasta to pan and simmer 2 minutes. Serve with Parmesan cheese.

Penne with Sautéed Chicken in White Wine
(4 servings)

1 ½	boneless chicken breasts, skinned	1 ½
3 tbsp	olive oil	45 mL
1 cup	dry white wine	250 mL
2	anchovy fillets, drained and chopped	2
2	garlic cloves, peeled, crushed and chopped	2
1 tbsp	chopped fresh basil	15 mL
¼ tsp	savory	1 mL
4	tomatoes, peeled, seeded and chopped	4
1 lb	penne, cooked al dente	450 g
½ cup	pitted black olives, sliced	125 mL
	salt and pepper	
	grated Parmesan cheese	

1 Slice chicken breasts into strips 1 in (2.5 cm) wide. Heat oil in sauté pan over medium heat. Add chicken strips and cook 4 minutes over high heat. Turn pieces over, season and continue cooking 4 minutes. Remove chicken from pan and set aside.

2 Add wine to hot pan and cook 2 minutes over high heat. Add anchovies, garlic, seasonings and tomatoes. Mix and cook 20 minutes over medium-low heat.

3 Add chicken to sauce and simmer 3 minutes over low heat. Mix in hot pasta and olives; simmer another 3 minutes.

4 Sprinkle with grated Parmesan cheese and serve.

Spaghetti with Shrimp and Mussels
(4 servings)

3 tbsp	olive oil	45 mL
I	onion, peeled and finely chopped	I
I	carrot, pared and diced	I
¾ lb	fresh mushrooms, cleaned and chopped	350 g
2	garlic cloves, peeled, crushed and chopped	2
I cup	dry white wine	250 mL
3	tomatoes, peeled, seeded and coarsely chopped	3
½ lb	shrimp, peeled and deveined	225 g
2 lb	steamed mussels, shelled	900 g
¾ lb	spaghetti, cooked al dente	350 g
I tbsp	chopped fresh parsley	15 mL
	salt and pepper	

1 Heat oil in sauté pan over medium heat. Add onion and carrot; season and cook 5 minutes. Add mushrooms and garlic; continue cooking 4 minutes over medium heat.

2 Pour in wine and cook 3 minutes. Stir in tomatoes and season well. Cook 6 minutes.

3 Add shrimp, correct seasoning and cook 2 minutes. Mix in mussels and cook I minute.

4 Add hot pasta, toss and simmer 2 minutes over low heat. Sprinkle with parsley and serve.

Fettuccine and Fresh Watercress
(4 servings)

¼ cup	olive oil	50 mL
4	shallots, peeled and chopped	4
2	garlic cloves, peeled, crushed and chopped	2
2 tbsp	brandy	30 mL
1	bunch watercress, washed and dried	1
1 lb	fettuccine, cooked al dente	450 g
	salt and pepper	
	grated Parmesan cheese	

1 Heat 2 tbsp (30 mL) oil in frying pan over medium heat. Add shallots and garlic; cook 3 minutes over low heat.

2 Add brandy and cook 20 seconds. Remove shallots from pan and set aside.

3 Return pan to stove over high heat. Add remaining oil and when hot, add watercress. Cook 1 minute over high heat.

4 Add hot pasta to pan and reduce heat to low. Add shallots and garlic, toss well and season.

5 Accompany with Parmesan cheese.

Hearty Eggplant Lasagne
(6 servings)

3	eggplants	3
1/3 cup	olive oil	75 mL
1 lb	lasagne, cooked al dente	450 g
2 1/2 cups	meat sauce, heated	625 mL
1 cup	grated mozzarella cheese	250 mL
2 1/2 cups	White Sauce, heated (see p. 86)	625 mL
1 1/4 cups	grated Parmesan cheese	300 mL
	salt and pepper	

Preheat oven to 350°F (180°C).

1 Cut eggplants into slices 1/4 in (5 mm) thick. Do not peel. Arrange slices flat on cookie sheet and sprinkle with salt. Let stand 1 hour at room temperature. Drain off liquid and pat dry.

2 Heat some of olive oil in large frying pan over medium heat. Sear eggplant slices in several batches, 2 minutes on each side.

3 Cover bottom of buttered lasagne baking dish with first layer of noodles. Add a layer of eggplant slices. Follow with layers of meat sauce, mozzarella, white sauce and Parmesan cheese. Season well between layers.

4 Repeat layers, ending with Parmesan cheese. Bake 40 minutes in oven. Let stand 5 minutes before serving.

Ricotta Spinach Lasagne
(6 servings)

2 lb	fresh spinach	900 g
4 tbsp	butter	60 mL
¾ lb	ricotta cheese	350 g
1 lb	lasagne, cooked al dente	450 g
4½ cups	White Sauce, heated (see p. 86)	1.1 L
1 cup	grated Parmesan cheese	250 mL
	salt and pepper	
	pinch of nutmeg	
	pinch of paprika	

Preheat oven to 350°F (180°C).

1 Remove stems from spinach. Wash leaves and cook in small amount of boiling water until wilted and soft. Transfer spinach to sieve and squeeze out excess water by pressing leaves with back of spoon. Chop spinach.

2 Heat butter in sauté pan over medium heat. Add spinach, season and cook 3 minutes.

3 Place ricotta cheese in bowl. Add spinach, season and mix well.

4 Cover bottom of buttered lasagne baking dish with a layer of noodles. Spread half of spinach/cheese mixture evenly over noodles.

5 Season white sauce with nutmeg and paprika. Spoon layer over spinach/cheese mixture. Sprinkle with Parmesan cheese.

6 Repeat layers, ending with Parmesan cheese. Bake 40 minutes in oven. Let stand 5 minutes before serving.

Spaghetti Tossed in Hot Olive Oil with Garlic
(4 servings)

3 tbsp	olive oil	45 mL
4	garlic cloves, peeled	4
1 lb	spaghetti, cooked al dente	450 g
1 tbsp	chopped fresh parsley	15 mL
¼ tsp	crushed chilies	1 mL
1 tbsp	chopped lemon zest	15 mL
	salt and pepper	
	grated Asiago cheese	

1 Pour olive oil into frying pan over low heat. Add garlic cloves and cook 2 minutes to flavor oil. Remove garlic from pan, chop finely and set aside.

2 Add hot spaghetti to oil in frying pan. Add garlic, parsley, crushed chilies and lemon zest. Mix well and season with salt and pepper.

3 Cook pasta 1 minute then serve with grated cheese.

Quick Chicken Sauté over Pasta
(4 servings)

1½	boneless chicken breasts, skinned	1½
5 tbsp	olive oil	75 mL
1½ cups	dry white wine	375 mL
½ cup	chopped fresh basil	125 mL
1 lb	pasta, cooked al dente	450 g
	salt and pepper	
	grated cheese	

1 Slice chicken into strips 1 in (2.5 cm) thick. Heat 3 tbsp (45 mL) oil in sauté pan over medium heat. Add chicken, season well and cook 3 minutes. Turn pieces over and continue cooking 3 minutes. Remove chicken from pan and set aside.

2 Add wine to hot pan. Cook over high heat to reduce by half. Add basil and remaining oil to pan. Add hot pasta and mix.

3 Return chicken to pan with pasta. Simmer 2 to 3 minutes over low heat.

4 Sprinkle with grated cheese and serve.

Spaghetti in Roasted Bell Pepper Sauce
(4 servings)

I	yellow bell pepper	I
I	red bell pepper	I
½	green bell pepper	½
2 tbsp	olive oil	30 mL
3	garlic cloves, peeled, crushed and chopped	3
I tsp	chili powder	5 mL
3	tomatoes, peeled, seeded and chopped	3
2 tbsp	chopped fresh basil	30 mL
I lb	spaghetti, cooked al dente	450 g
	salt and pepper	
	grated Romano cheese	

1 Cut bell peppers in half and remove seeds. Oil skin and place cut-side-down on cookie sheet; broil 6 minutes in oven. Remove from oven and let cool. Peel off skin, slice peppers and set aside.

2 Heat oil in frying pan over medium heat. Add sliced peppers, garlic and chili powder. Reduce heat to low and cook 5 minutes. Stir 2 to 3 times during cooking.

3 Add tomatoes and basil; season well. Cook 10 minutes over medium heat. Do not cover.

4 Ladle sauce over hot pasta and serve with Romano cheese.

Spaghetti with Pesto
(4 servings)

3 cups	fresh basil, washed and dried	750 mL
¼ cup	pine nuts	50 mL
3 tbsp	chopped fresh parsley	45 mL
5	garlic cloves, peeled, crushed and chopped	5
½ cup	Parmesan cheese	125 mL
½ cup	olive oil	125 mL
1 lb	spaghetti, cooked al dente	450 g
	salt and pepper	

1 Place all ingredients, except oil and pasta, in food processor. Blend 1 minute.

2 While machine is blending, pour oil in thin stream through hole in top to incorporate. Transfer mixture to large bowl.

3 Toss hot pasta with pesto mixture. Serve with more cheese, if desired.

Penne à la Diable
(4 servings)

1 tbsp	olive oil	15 mL
2 oz	bacon, diced	60 g
¾ lb	fresh mushrooms, cleaned and sliced	350 g
1	red bell pepper, diced	1
2	garlic cloves, peeled, crushed and chopped	2
4	tomatoes, peeled, quartered and seeded	4
2 tbsp	chopped fresh basil	30 mL
1 lb	penne, cooked al dente	450 g
	salt and pepper	
	grated Parmesan and Pecorino cheeses	

1 Heat oil in frying pan over medium heat. Add bacon and cook 6 minutes. Remove bacon from pan and set aside.

2 Add mushrooms to pan, season and cook 4 minutes over high heat. Remove mushrooms from pan and set aside.

3 Add red pepper and garlic to pan. Cook 3 minutes over medium heat. As soon as garlic becomes golden in color, remove garlic and red pepper from pan; set aside.

4 Add tomatoes, basil, salt and pepper to pan. Cook 10 minutes over medium heat. Return bacon, mushrooms, garlic and red pepper to pan with tomatoes. Season well and cook 1 minute.

5 Place hot penne in serving platter. Sprinkle grated cheeses over pasta and cover with sauce. Serve.

Pork Tenderloin and Pasta Stir-Fry
(4 servings)

3 tbsp	olive oil	45 mL
1	pork tenderloin, fat removed and sliced ½ in (1 cm) thick	1
½	celery stalk, sliced	½
1	yellow bell pepper, thinly sliced	1
1	green bell pepper, thinly sliced	1
1	small chili pepper, chopped	1
2	garlic cloves, peeled, crushed and chopped	2
½ cup	dry white wine	125 mL
½ cup	pine nuts	125 mL
¾ lb	penne or shells, cooked al dente	350 g
½ cup	grated Asiago cheese	125 mL
	salt and pepper	

1 Heat oil in sauté pan over medium heat. Add pork and cook 2 minutes. Turn pieces over, season and cook 2 minutes. Remove meat from pan and set aside.

2 Add celery, bell peppers and chili pepper to pan. Add garlic and cook 4 minutes over high heat. Season well, pour in wine and continue cooking 2 minutes.

3 Return pork to pan. Add pine nuts and hot pasta. Mix well and add half of cheese. Mix, season and simmer 2 minutes.

4 Serve with remaining cheese.

Tortellini with Garlic Chicken Sauce
(4 servings)

1	red bell pepper	1
3 tbsp	butter	45 mL
4	garlic cloves, peeled, crushed and chopped	4
10	fresh basil leaves, chopped	10
3 tbsp	flour	45 mL
2 cups	chicken stock, heated	500 mL
1 lb	tortellini, cooked al dente	450 g
⅓ cup	grated Parmesan cheese	75 mL
	salt and pepper	

1 Cut bell pepper in half and remove seeds. Oil skin and place cut-side-down on cookie sheet; broil 6 minutes in oven. Remove from oven and let cool. Peel off skin and dice.

2 Heat butter in sauté pan over medium heat. Add garlic and basil; cook 2 minutes. Sprinkle in flour, mix and cook 1 minute.

3 Pour in chicken stock and whisk to incorporate. Season and cook sauce 6 minutes over medium heat.

4 Add pasta to sauce in pan. Toss and incorporate half of cheese. Stir in diced bell pepper and simmer 2 minutes over low heat.

5 Serve with remaining cheese.

Macaroni Niçoise
(4 servings)

I	bunch fresh asparagus	I
I	small head broccoli	I
7 oz	can tuna, packed in water, drained	198 g
1 1/2 cups	cooked macaroni	375 mL
2	hard-boiled eggs, quartered	2
1/2	red onion, sliced in rings	1/2
I	tomato, cored and cut in wedges	I
1 tbsp	Dijon mustard	15 mL
3 tbsp	wine vinegar	45 mL
9 tbsp	olive oil	135 mL
2 tbsp	chopped fresh basil	30 mL
I cup	diced mozzarella cheese	250 mL
	salt and pepper	
	pitted black olives	

1 Pare asparagus stalks if necessary and trim stem ends. Blanch in salted, boiling water 3 to 4 minutes, or adjust time depending on size. Drain well, let cool and cut stalks into 1-in (2.5-cm) lengths.

2 Separate head of broccoli into florets. Blanch 2 to 3 minutes in salted, boiling water. Drain well and let cool.

3 Flake tuna and place in large bowl. Add asparagus and broccoli. Add pasta, eggs, red onion and tomato. Season well.

4 Place mustard, vinegar, salt and pepper in small bowl. Whisk together. Add oil in thin stream, whisking constantly. Add basil to vinaigrette, whisk and correct seasoning.

5 Pour vinaigrette over salad ingredients and mix well. Serve on lettuce leaves and top with diced mozzarella and olives.

Penne in Mushroom Red Wine Sauce
(4 servings)

1 ½ cups	dry red wine	375 mL
1	bay leaf	1
3 tbsp	butter	45 mL
2	large shallots, peeled and finely chopped	2
2	garlic cloves, peeled, crushed and finely chopped	2
¾ lb	fresh mushrooms, cleaned and sliced	350 g
3 tbsp	flour	45 mL
1 ½ cups	beef stock, heated	375 mL
1 lb	penne, cooked al dente	450 g
1 tbsp	chopped fresh parsley	15 mL
	salt and pepper	
	grated Asiago or Parmesan cheese	

1 Pour wine into saucepan with bay leaf. Cook over medium heat until reduced by ⅓. Discard bay leaf.

2 Heat butter in frying pan over medium heat. Add shallots and garlic; cook 3 minutes. Add mushrooms, season well and continue cooking 4 minutes.

3 Mix in flour and cook 2 minutes over medium-low heat. Pour in beef stock and mix well. Continue cooking sauce 3 minutes.

4 Mix in reduced wine; cook 8 minutes over low heat. Correct seasoning.

5 Place hot pasta in mixing bowl. Pour in sauce and mix well. Sprinkle in parsley and cheese. Mix and serve.

Fettuccine in Anchovy Tomato Sauce
(4 servings)

1 tbsp	olive oil	15 mL
1	onion, peeled and finely chopped	1
3	garlic cloves, peeled, crushed and chopped	3
1	shallot, peeled and finely chopped	1
28 oz	can tomatoes, drained and chopped	796 mL
6	anchovy fillets, drained and chopped	6
1/2 cup	pitted black olives, sliced	125 mL
1/4 tsp	crushed chilies	1 mL
2 tbsp	chopped fresh basil	30 mL
1 lb	fettuccine, cooked al dente	450 g
	salt and pepper	
	grated Pecorino Sardo cheese	

1 Heat oil in frying pan over medium heat. Add onion, garlic and shallot; cook 3 minutes over low heat.

2 Add tomatoes and season well. Cook 10 minutes over medium-low heat.

3 Add remaining ingredients to frying pan, except pasta and cheese, and mix well. Simmer sauce 5 minutes over low heat.

4 Place hot fettuccine in bowl and add sauce. Mix until evenly coated and sprinkle servings with cheese.

Rigatoni in Curry Sauce with Apples
(4 servings)

3 tbsp	butter	45 mL
I	onion, peeled and finely chopped	I
2	garlic cloves, peeled, crushed and chopped	2
⅓	celery stalk, diced	⅓
I	carrot, pared and diced	I
I	small red chili pepper, seeded and chopped	I
3 tbsp	curry powder	45 mL
3 tbsp	flour	45 mL
2½ cups	chicken stock, heated	625 mL
I	large cooking apple, cored, peeled and diced	I
I tbsp	chopped fresh parsley	15 mL
¼ cup	heavy cream (optional)	50 mL
I lb	rigatoni, cooked al dente	450 g
	salt and pepper	

1 Heat butter in sauté pan over medium heat. Add onion, garlic and celery; mix and cook 3 minutes. Add carrot and chili pepper; continue cooking 4 minutes.

2 Mix in curry powder and cook 4 minutes over low heat. Add flour, mix and continue cooking I minute.

3 Whisk in chicken stock and season well. Cook sauce 14 minutes over medium heat.

4 Add apple, parsley and cream. Cook 4 minutes over low heat. Add hot pasta to sauce and toss well. Simmer 2 minutes, then serve with grated cheese, if desired.

Spaetzle (German Noodles)
(4 to 6 servings)

3 cups	all-purpose flour	750 mL
2	large eggs, beaten	2
1 tsp	salt	5 mL
2 tbsp	cold water	30 mL
1 tsp	olive oil	5 mL
1 cup	grated Gruyère cheese	250 mL
	salt and pepper	

Preheat oven to 350°F (180°C).

1 Mound flour on work surface and make well in center. Add beaten eggs, salt and water to well. Slowly incorporate ingredients into flour, being careful not to break down walls of well. If needed, add more water. The dough should be quite soft.

2 Cut dough into 4 pieces and roll each piece ¼ in (5 mm) thick. Cut dough into small pieces. Cook in boiling, salted water with 1 tsp (5 mL) oil for 5 to 6 minutes.

3 Drain noodles well and mix with half of cheese. Season very well with pepper and place in buttered baking dish. Top with remaining cheese and bake 15 minutes in oven. Serve with a beef stew.

Pasta Pollo with Roasted Peppers
(4 servings)

2	whole boneless chicken breasts, skinned	2
¼ cup	flour	50 mL
3	bell peppers	3
3 tbsp	olive oil	45 mL
1	onion, peeled and thinly sliced	1
2	garlic cloves, peeled, crushed and chopped	2
2 tbsp	chopped fresh basil	30 mL
½ cup	chicken stock, heated	125 mL
3 tbsp	Marsala wine	45 mL
1 lb	pasta, cooked al dente	450 g
	salt and pepper	
	chopped fresh parsley	

1 Slice chicken breasts into strips 1 in (2.5 cm) wide. Season meat well, then dredge pieces in flour; set aside.

2 Cut bell peppers in half and remove seeds. Oil skin and place cut-side-down on cookie sheet; broil 6 minutes in oven. Remove from oven and let cool. Peel off skin and slice thinly.

3 Heat oil in sauté pan over medium heat. Add onion and garlic; cook 4 minutes.

4 Add chicken pieces and season. Continue cooking 6 minutes over medium heat. Add basil and chicken stock; cook 3 minutes over low heat.

5 Pour in wine and add peppers and hot pasta. Toss and simmer 2 minutes over low heat.

6 Sprinkle with chopped fresh parsley before serving.

Rigatoni Baked with Virginia Ham
(4 servings)

3	large eggs, separated	3
¼ cup	melted butter	50 mL
1 ¼ cups	sour cream	300 mL
¾ lb	rigatoni, cooked al dente	350 g
½ lb	cooked Virginia ham, diced	225 g
	freshly ground pepper	

Preheat oven to 350°F (180°C).

1 Place egg yolks in large bowl. Add melted butter and sour cream; mix well. Season with pepper and mix again.

2 Add hot pasta to egg yolk mixture; mix well. Set aside.

3 Place egg whites in stainless steel bowl and beat until stiff. Incorporate egg whites into pasta mixture. Season well with pepper.

4 Place half of pasta in bottom of buttered baking dish. Add ham in an even layer and cover with remaining pasta. Bake 20 minutes in oven. Garnish with sliced pitted black olives, if desired.

Fettuccine Supreme
(4 servings)

3 tbsp	olive oil	45 mL
2 oz	diced Virginia ham	60 g
3	garlic cloves, peeled, crushed and chopped	3
3	tomatoes, peeled, seeded and chopped	3
1/2 lb	fresh mushrooms, cleaned and halved	225 g
1/2 lb	chicken livers, cleaned and halved	225 g
1/2 cup	dry white wine	125 mL
I cup	chicken stock, heated	250 mL
1/2 cup	chopped fresh basil	125 mL
I lb	fettuccine, cooked al dente	450 g
	salt and pepper	
	grated cheese	

1 Heat half of oil in sauté pan over medium heat. Add ham and garlic; cook 3 minutes. Add tomatoes and season well. Cook 8 minutes over high heat. Remove contents from pan and set aside.

2 Add remaining oil to hot pan. When hot, add mushrooms and chicken livers; season well. Cook 3 minutes over high heat. Pour in wine and continue cooking 2 minutes.

3 Add chicken stock and cook 4 minutes. Return tomato and chicken livers mixture to pan and add basil. Mix well.

4 Add hot pasta and toss. Simmer 2 minutes and serve with grated cheese.

Linguine with Fresh Mussels in Tomato Sauce
(4 servings)

4 lb	fresh mussels, bearded and scrubbed	1.8 kg
6	shallots, peeled and finely chopped	6
2 tbsp	chopped fresh parsley	30 mL
½ cup	dry white wine	125 mL
2 tbsp	butter	30 mL
1	garlic clove, peeled, crushed and chopped	1
2 tsp	chopped chili pepper	10 mL
15	fresh basil leaves	15
1½ cups	tomato sauce, heated	375 mL
1 lb	linguine, cooked al dente	450 g
	salt and pepper	

1 Place mussels in large pot. Add half of shallots, all of parsley and wine. Cover and bring to boil. Cook mussels over low heat until shells open, about 5 minutes. Stir once during cooking.

2 Remove mussels from pot, discarding any unopened shells. Set aside 12 mussels in the shell; keep warm. Remove remaining mussels from shells and set aside.

3 Strain cooking liquid from mussels through sieve lined with cheesecloth into small saucepan. Cook 5 minutes over high heat to reduce liquid by ⅔.

4 Meanwhile, heat butter in frying pan over medium heat. Add remaining shallots and garlic. Cook 2 minutes. Add chili pepper, basil and reduced cooking liquid. Mix well and cook 2 minutes. Season to taste.

5 Incorporate hot tomato sauce and cook 6 minutes over low heat. Place shelled mussels in sauce, mix and add hot pasta. Mix and simmer briefly.

6 Serve pasta decorated with mussels in the shell.

Sauté of Shrimp with Pasta
(4 servings)

4 tbsp	olive oil	60 mL
1 lb	shrimp, peeled and deveined	450 g
3	garlic cloves, peeled, crushed and chopped	3
3 tbsp	chopped fresh parsley	45 mL
1 tbsp	chopped chili pepper (optional)	15 mL
⅓ cup	chicken stock, heated	75 mL
1 lb	pasta, cooked al dente	450 g
	salt and pepper	
	few drops of lemon juice	

1 Heat oil in large frying pan over medium heat. Add shrimp and cook 2 minutes. Turn shrimp over and continue cooking 2 minutes.

2 Season with salt and pepper. Add garlic, parsley, chili pepper and chicken stock. Cook 2 minutes.

3 Add hot pasta and toss. Simmer 2 minutes over low heat. Add a few drops of lemon juice, correct seasoning and serve.

Fusilli Salad with Rouille Dressing
(4 to 6 servings)

1	red bell pepper	1
1/2 lb	fusilli, cooked al dente	225 g
3	garlic cloves, peeled, crushed and chopped	3
1 1/4 cups	frozen corn, cooked	300 mL
2	tomatoes, peeled, seeded and diced	2
1/2 cup	pitted black olives, sliced	125 mL
1 cup	grated pared carrots	250 mL
3	green onions, chopped	3
1/2 cup	Rouille Dressing (see p. 91)	125 mL
	salt and pepper	
	juice of 1/2 lemon	
	grated Pecorino cheese	

1 Cut bell pepper in half and remove seeds. Oil skin and place cut-side-down on cookie sheet; broil 6 minutes in oven. Remove from oven and let cool. Peel off skin and dice.

2 Place diced pepper in large bowl. Add remaining ingredients, except dressing, lemon juice and cheese, to bowl.

3 Add dressing and lemon juice; mix well. Correct seasoning and sprinkle with grated Pecorino cheese.

Baked Cannelloni
(4 servings)

1 tbsp	olive oil	15 mL
2	shallots, peeled and chopped	2
½ cup	dry white wine	125 mL
4	tomatoes, peeled, seeded and chopped	4
2 tbsp	chopped fresh basil	30 mL
8	stuffed cannelloni, ready to bake	8
6-8	slices mozzarella cheese	6-8
	salt and pepper	

Preheat oven to 350°F (180°C).

1 Heat oil in frying pan over medium heat. Add shallots and cook 2 minutes. Pour in wine, increase heat to high and cook 2 minutes.

2 Stir in tomatoes and basil; season well. Cook 5 minutes over medium heat.

3 Arrange single layer of stuffed cannelloni in buttered baking dish. Pour in tomato sauce and cover with slices of cheese.

4 Bake 20 minutes in oven.

Seafood Pasta Salad
(4 servings)

1 tbsp	Dijon mustard	15 mL
1	shallot, peeled and chopped	1
1	garlic clove, peeled, crushed and chopped	1
1 tbsp	chopped fresh tarragon	15 mL
3 tbsp	wine vinegar	45 mL
9 tbsp	olive oil	135 mL
½ lb	large shrimp, cooked	225 g
½ lb	pasta, cooked al dente	225 g
1	apple, cored and sliced with skin	1
3	green onions, sliced	3
3	bamboo shoots, sliced ¼ in (5 mm) thick	3
½ cup	pitted olives, sliced	125 mL
1	small head broccoli, florets blanched	1
1	carrot, pared and grated	1
	salt and pepper	
	juice of ½ lemon	
	lettuce leaves	

1 Place mustard, shallot, garlic, tarragon and vinegar in bowl. Season with salt and pepper; whisk to incorporate. Add oil in thin stream, whisking constantly. Season and add lemon juice.

2 Peel and devein shrimp. Place in large bowl. Add remaining salad ingredients, except lettuce, and mix well.

3 Pour dressing over salad and toss to combine. Correct seasoning and serve on lettuce leaves.

Rigatoni with Salmon in White Sauce
(4 servings)

2	medium salmon steaks	2
2 tbsp	olive oil	30 mL
2	garlic cloves, peeled, crushed and chopped	2
3	fresh basil leaves	3
¾ lb	rigatoni, cooked	350 g
2 cups	White Sauce, heated (see p. 86)	500 mL
¼ lb	mozzarella, cubed	125 g
	salt and pepper	

1 Place salmon steaks in baking dish. Mix oil with garlic; pour over salmon. Add basil leaves and marinate 1 hour in refrigerator.

2 Transfer salmon steaks to ovenproof tray. Broil 8 to 10 minutes in oven, turning steaks over once during cooking. When cooked, remove salmon from oven and let cool. Remove bones and flake fish with a fork.

3 Preheat oven to 375°F (190°C).

4 Place pasta, salmon and hot white sauce in mixing bowl. Season well and mix until combined.

5 Pour pasta mixture into buttered baking dish. Season well and cover with cubed mozzarella. Bake 10 minutes in oven.

Baked Cappelletti – Bohemian Style
(4 servings)

5 tbsp	olive oil	75 mL
2	medium eggplants, peeled and diced	2
3	tomatoes, peeled, seeded and diced	3
2	garlic cloves, peeled	2
1 tbsp	chopped fresh parsley	15 mL
¹/₂ tsp	oregano	2 mL
3	anchovy fillets, drained and chopped	3
1 tbsp	flour	15 mL
¹/₄ cup	milk	50 mL
¹/₄ cup	white breadcrumbs	50 mL
³/₄ lb	cappelletti, cooked al dente	350 g
6 to 8	slices Fontina cheese	6 to 8
	salt and pepper	

1 Heat 4 tbsp (60 mL) oil in frying pan over medium heat. Add eggplant and season well. Cook 15 minutes or until eggplant turns golden.

2 Add tomatoes, whole garlic cloves, parsley and oregano; season well. Cook 20 minutes over medium heat, stirring frequently.

3 Preheat oven to 375°F (190°C).

4 Heat remaining oil in small saucepan over medium heat. Add anchovies and cook 2 minutes. Stir in flour, then pour in milk. Mix and cook 2 minutes. Add breadcrumbs and mix well.

5 Remove garlic cloves from eggplant sauce. Add anchovy mixture to sauce and mix to incorporate.

6 Toss hot pasta with eggplant sauce. Place in buttered baking dish and cover with Fontina cheese. Bake 15 minutes in oven.

Summer Harvest Pasta
(4 servings)

3 tbsp	butter	45 mL
1	carrot, pared and cut in julienne	1
½	celery stalk, cut in julienne	½
1	leek, white part only, cleaned and thinly sliced	1
1	small red chili pepper, seeded and chopped	1
½ cup	chicken stock, heated	125 mL
¾ cup	heavy cream	175 mL
1 lb	spaghetti, cooked al dente	450 g
½ cup	green peas, cooked	125 mL
½ cup	grated Fontina cheese	125 mL
	salt and pepper	

1 Heat butter in large sauté pan over medium heat. Add carrot, celery, leek and chili pepper; season well. Cover and cook 3 minutes over low heat.

2 Remove vegetables from pan and set aside. Add chicken stock and cream to hot pan; season well. Cook 3 minutes over high heat.

3 Add hot pasta and vegetables, including peas, to sauce in pan. Toss and simmer 2 minutes. Add cheese, mix and simmer 1 minute.

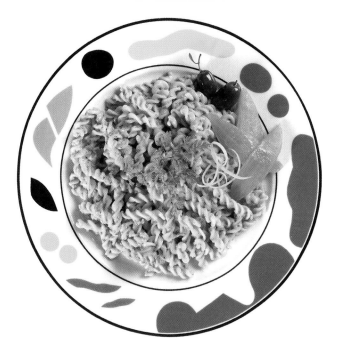

Fusilli Tapenade
(4 servings)

¹⁄₃ lb	**pitted black olives**	150 g
¹⁄₃ lb	**capers**	150 g
3 oz	**anchovy fillets, drained**	90 g
3 oz	**tuna, packed in oil, drained**	90 g
1 tsp	**powdered mustard**	5 mL
3	**garlic cloves, peeled, crushed and chopped**	3
¹⁄₂ cup	**olive oil**	125 mL
1 lb	**fusilli, cooked al dente**	450 g
¹⁄₂ cup	**cooking liquid from pasta**	125 mL
	pinch of nutmeg	
	lemon juice to taste	
	salt and freshly ground pepper	
	grated Parmesan cheese	

1 Place olives, capers, anchovies, tuna, mustard, garlic and nutmeg in food processor; blend 30 seconds. While machine is blending, add oil in thin stream through hole in top.

2 Transfer mixture to bowl. Add lemon juice to taste and season well.

3 Place hot pasta in sauté pan. Add anchovy tapenade and mix well. Stir in a little cooking liquid from pasta to help incorporate tapenade.

4 Serve with Parmesan cheese.

Toasted Walnut Pasta Salad
(4 servings)

2	**Belgian endives**	2
1	**small head chicory**	1
1 ½ cups	**pasta, cooked al dente**	375 mL
2	**apples, cored, peeled and diced**	2
½ cup	**toasted walnut pieces**	125 mL
2	**egg yolks**	2
2 tbsp	**lemon juice**	30 mL
¾ cup	**olive oil**	175 mL
	salt and pepper	

1 Core endives and separate leaves. Wash well and dry. Cut leaves into pieces ½ in (1 cm) wide. Place in large bowl.

2 Wash chicory well and dry. Tear leaves into small pieces and add to bowl. Toss in pasta, apples and walnut pieces.

3 Place egg yolks in small bowl. Add salt, pepper and lemon juice. Whisk together.

4 Incorporate oil in thin stream, whisking constantly. If mayonnaise becomes too thick, add a little more lemon juice.

5 Correct seasoning and mix mayonnaise with pasta salad.

Fruity Noodles with Pecorino Cream Sauce

(4 servings)

3 tbsp	butter	45 mL
2	small apples, cored, peeled and diced	2
3	egg yolks	3
¼ cup	heavy cream	50 mL
½ cup	grated Pecorino cheese	125 mL
1 lb	broad egg noodles, cooked al dente	450 g
	pinch nutmeg	
	salt and freshly ground pepper	
	pinch paprika	

1 Heat 2 tbsp (30 mL) butter in frying pan over medium heat. Add apples and cook 4 minutes over high heat.

2 Meanwhile, beat egg yolks and cream together in mixing bowl. Add cheese and all seasonings.

3 Melt remaining butter in frying pan over low heat. Add hot noodles and coat with butter. Season well and add egg yolk/cream mixture. Mix quickly over low heat until well coated. Do not boil. Serve.

Insalata of Farfalle with Tuna
(4 servings)

¹/₂ lb	farfalle*, cooked al dente	225 g
1 ¹/₂ cups	cooked white beans	375 mL
¹/₂ cup	pitted black olives, sliced	125 mL
1	garlic clove, peeled, crushed and chopped	1
2 tbsp	chopped fresh parsley	30 mL
2 tbsp	chopped fresh basil	30 mL
¹/₃ cup	olive oil	75 mL
4	anchovy fillets, drained and mashed	4
1 tbsp	capers	15 mL
¹/₄ lb	tuna, packed in oil, drained and flaked	125 g
¹/₄ lb	fresh crabmeat, cooked	125 g
	salt and freshly ground pepper	
	lemon juice to taste	

1 Place pasta, beans, olives, garlic, parsley and basil in large bowl. Season with pepper.

2 Heat oil in frying pan over low heat. Add anchovies and mix with wooden spoon to form paste.

3 Add capers and lemon juice to anchovies. Pour half of mixture over salad ingredients in bowl. Mix well.

4 Make well in center of salad ingredients. Add tuna and crabmeat to well. Pour remaining anchovy mixture over, correct seasoning and serve salad.

* Farfalle is a bow-tie shaped pasta.

Ravioli in Sun-Dried Tomato Sauce
(4 servings)

2 tbsp	olive oil	30 mL
2	shallots, peeled and finely chopped	2
1/2	celery stalk, diced	1/2
1	carrot, pared and diced	1
3	garlic cloves, peeled, crushed and chopped	3
4	tomatoes, peeled, seeded and chopped	4
1 tbsp	chopped fresh basil	15 mL
1/2 tsp	oregano	2 mL
1/4 cup	sun-dried tomatoes, chopped	50 mL
1 lb	meat-stuffed ravioli, cooked	450 g
	salt and pepper	
	grated Pecorino cheese	

1 Heat oil in frying pan over medium heat. Add shallots, celery, carrot and garlic; cook 6 minutes over low heat.

2 Add fresh tomatoes and seasonings. Increase heat to medium and cook 6 minutes.

3 Stir in sun-dried tomatoes; continue cooking 4 minutes.

4 Correct seasoning and add hot pasta to sauce in pan. Mix and simmer 4 minutes over low heat.

5 Serve with grated cheese.

Quick Spaghetti and Clams in Red Sauce
(4 servings)

3 tbsp	olive oil	45 mL
1	onion, peeled and chopped	1
4	garlic cloves, peeled, crushed and chopped	4
1/2	celery stalk, diced	1/2
28 oz	can plum tomatoes, drained and chopped	796 mL
1 tbsp	chopped fresh basil	15 mL
1 tbsp	chopped fresh parsley	15 mL
2	5 oz (142 g) cans baby clams, drained and chopped (reserve juice)	2
1 lb	spaghetti, cooked al dente	450 g
	pinch of sugar	
	salt and pepper	
	grated Pecorino cheese	

1 Heat oil in sauté pan over medium heat. Add onion, garlic and celery; cook 5 minutes.

2 Add tomatoes, sugar, basil, parsley and reserved clam juice. Season well and bring to boil. Cook 30 minutes over low heat.

3 Stir chopped clams into sauce and simmer 3 minutes over low heat. Serve sauce over hot pasta with Pecorino cheese.

Spaghetti with Ratatouille Sauce
(4 servings)

2 tbsp	olive oil	30 mL
3	garlic cloves, peeled, crushed and chopped	3
1	onion, peeled and chopped	1
1/2 cup	dry white wine	125 mL
1	medium eggplant, peeled and diced	1
4	tomatoes, peeled, seeded and diced	4
2 tbsp	chopped fresh basil	30 mL
1/2 tsp	oregano	2 mL
1/4 tsp	chili pepper	1 mL
1	green bell pepper, diced	1
1 lb	spaghetti, cooked al dente	450 g
	salt and pepper	
	grated cheese	

1 Heat oil in frying pan over medium heat. Add garlic and onion; cook 3 minutes. Pour in wine and continue cooking 3 minutes.

2 Add eggplant, tomatoes and seasonings. Bring to boil, cover and cook 40 minutes over low heat. Stir frequently and add water as required if cooking liquid evaporates.

3 Ten minutes before end of cooking time, stir in diced green pepper.

4 Serve ratatouille over hot pasta and accompany with grated cheese.

Linguine with Light Basil Sauce
(4 servings)

1 ½ cups	fresh basil, washed and dried	375 mL
3	garlic cloves, peeled, crushed and chopped	3
½ cup	grated Parmesan cheese	125 mL
½ cup	olive oil	125 mL
¼ cup	white breadcrumbs	50 mL
¼ cup	pine nuts	50 mL
1 lb	linguine, cooked al dente	450 g
¼ cup	cooking liquid from pasta	50 mL
	salt and pepper	

1 Place basil and garlic in food processor; blend 30 seconds.

2 Add cheese and blend 10 seconds. Add half of oil and blend another 30 seconds.

3 Add breadcrumbs, pine nuts and remaining oil. Blend 30 seconds and season well.

4 Drain hot pasta and return to saucepan in which it was cooked. Add ¼ cup (50 mL) reserved cooking liquid and mix well. Stir in basil mixture. Cook 1 minute over low heat.

5 Serve decorated with fresh basil leaves.

Ravioli in Gorgonzola Cream Sauce
(4 servings)

6 oz	Gorgonzola cheese, in small pieces	175 g
1 cup	heavy cream	250 mL
3 tbsp	melted butter	45 mL
1 lb	ravioli, cooked al dente	450 g
3 tbsp	grated Parmesan cheese	45 mL
	salt and pepper	
	paprika to taste	

1 Place cheese and heavy cream in sauté pan over low heat. Season well and add paprika. Cook 4 minutes until creamy.

2 Stir in butter and add hot pasta. Mix and simmer 1 minute over low heat.

3 Sprinkle with Parmesan cheese and serve.

Fusilli with Fresh Littleneck Clams
(4 servings)

36	littleneck clams, scrubbed	36
1 cup	water	250 mL
3 tbsp	olive oil	45 mL
3	garlic cloves, peeled, crushed and chopped	3
2	large tomatoes, peeled, quartered, seeded and chopped	2
28 oz	can tomatoes, drained and chopped	796 mL
2 tbsp	chopped fresh basil	30 mL
1 lb	fusilli, cooked al dente	450 g
¾ cup	grated Romano cheese	175 mL
	salt and freshly ground pepper	

1 Place clams in saucepan with water. Cover and bring to boil. Reduce heat and simmer 3 to 4 minutes.

2 Remove clams from pan, discarding any that did not open. Place pan, still containing liquid, on stove over medium heat. Reduce liquid by ½. Strain through cheesecloth and set aside.

3 Remove clams from shells and chop. Set aside.

4 Heat oil in frying pan over medium heat. Add garlic and cook 1 minute. Add fresh and canned tomatoes, basil and reserved liquid from clams. Season well and cook 12 minutes over high heat until mixture becomes thick.

5 Stir chopped clams into pasta sauce. Reheat 1 to 2 minutes.

6 Place hot pasta in heated serving bowl. Add grated cheese and mix well. Pour in clam sauce, mix, season with pepper and serve.

Penne with Hearts of Palm
(4 servings)

2 tbsp	butter	30 mL
3	shallots, peeled and finely chopped	3
14.5 oz	can hearts of palm, drained and sliced ¼ in (5 mm) thick	410 g
2 tbsp	chopped fresh basil	30 mL
1 cup	dry white wine	250 mL
3	tomatoes, peeled, seeded and coarsely chopped	3
1	small red chili pepper, halved	1
1 lb	penne, cooked al dente	450 g
½ cup	grated Parmesan cheese	125 mL
	salt and pepper	

1 Heat butter in sauté pan over medium heat. Add shallots and cook 1 minute. Add hearts of palm and basil; cook 3 minutes over low heat.

2 Pour in wine and cook 2 minutes over medium heat. Add tomatoes and drop in chili pepper. Season well. Cook sauce 15 minutes over medium heat.

3 Remove chili pepper and discard. Add hot pasta to sauce and mix well. Mix in half of cheese and simmer 3 minutes over low heat.

4 Serve with remaining cheese.

Egg Noodles in Ground Lamb Sauce
(4 servings)

2	green bell peppers	2
2½ tbsp	olive oil	40 mL
3	garlic cloves, peeled, crushed and chopped	3
2	shallots, peeled and chopped	2
¾ lb	lean ground lamb	350 g
I cup	dry white wine	250 mL
3	large tomatoes, peeled, seeded and chopped	3
I tbsp	chopped fresh parsley	15 mL
I lb	egg noodles, cooked al dente	450 g
	salt and pepper	

1 Cut bell peppers in half and remove seeds. Oil skin and place cut-side-down on cookie sheet; broil 6 minutes in oven. Remove from oven and let cool. Peel off skin, slice peppers thinly and set aside.

2 Heat oil in sauté pan over medium heat. Add garlic and shallots; cook 3 minutes over low heat.

3 Add ground lamb and season well. Mix and cook 7 minutes over medium heat. Add remaining ingredients, except pasta, and cook 16 minutes over low heat.

4 Add hot pasta to sauce in pan. Mix and season well. Simmer 3 minutes and serve.

Spaghetti with Chicken Livers
(4 servings)

4 tbsp	olive oil	60 mL
I	onion, peeled and chopped	I
4	garlic cloves, peeled, crushed and chopped	4
½ cup	dry red wine	125 mL
28 oz	can tomatoes, drained and chopped	796 mL
5½ oz	can tomato paste	156 mL
I tbsp	chili powder	15 mL
½ tsp	oregano	2 mL
¾ lb	chicken livers, cleaned and halved	350 g
¼ cup	red wine vinegar	50 mL
I lb	spaghetti, cooked al dente	450 g
	salt and pepper	

1 Heat half of oil in large sauté pan over medium heat. Add onion and half of garlic; cook 3 minutes.

2 Pour in wine and cook 2 minutes. Add tomatoes and tomato paste; mix well. Season and add chili powder and oregano. Cook sauce 35 minutes over low heat. Do not cover.

3 Heat remaining oil in frying pan over high heat. When hot, add chicken livers, season well and add remaining garlic. Cook 3 minutes over high heat. Remove contents from pan and set aside.

4 Place frying pan on stove over high heat. To deglaze pan, pour in vinegar and cook 2 minutes, scraping bottom of pan with wooden spoon. Pour contents of pan into tomato sauce.

5 Just before serving, place chicken livers in tomato sauce to reheat. Simmer 2 minutes over low heat.

6 Serve sauce ladled over hot pasta.

Ziti with Vegetables
(4 servings)

4 tbsp	olive oil	60 mL
I	onion, peeled and thinly sliced	I
2	garlic cloves, peeled, crushed and chopped	2
I	small zucchini, thinly sliced	I
¹⁄₃	eggplant, peeled and diced	¹⁄₃
I	red bell pepper, sliced	I
I	green bell pepper, sliced	I
I	large tomato, peeled, seeded and coarsely chopped	I
I lb	ziti, cooked al dente	450 g
2 tbsp	virgin olive oil	30 mL
8	fresh basil leaves	8
	salt and pepper	

1 Heat regular olive oil in sauté pan over medium heat. Add onion and cook 3 minutes. Add garlic and cook 1 minute.

2 Add remaining vegetables and season well. Cook 5 minutes over high heat, stirring once.

3 Place hot pasta in heated serving bowl. Toss with virgin olive oil and add vegetables. Mix and garnish servings with basil.

Fettuccine Jardinière

(4 servings)

2 tbsp	olive oil	30 mL
2	slices bacon, diced	2
2	green onions, diced	2
2	garlic cloves, peeled, crushed and chopped	2
½ cup	dry white wine	125 mL
1	carrot, pared and diced	1
1	zucchini, diced	1
1	green bell pepper, diced	1
3	tomatoes, peeled, seeded and diced	3
2 tbsp	chopped fresh basil	30 mL
1 lb	fettuccine, cooked al dente	450 g
1 cup	grated Parmesan cheese	250 mL
	salt and pepper	

1 Heat oil in large frying pan over medium heat. Add bacon and cook 4 minutes. Add green onions and garlic; continue cooking 3 minutes.

2 Pour in wine and cook 2 minutes. Add remaining vegetables and basil; season well. Cook 15 minutes over low heat. Do not cover.

3 Place hot pasta in serving bowl. Add cheese and mix well. Add vegetables and toss. Serve.

Pasta with Alfredo Sauce
(4 servings)

4 tbsp	butter	60 mL
I cup	heavy cream	250 mL
I lb	fettuccine or linguine, cooked al dente	450 g
¼ cup	grated Parmesan cheese	50 mL
	salt and pepper	
	paprika to taste	

1 Melt butter in sauté pan over low heat. Add heavy cream and season well; cook 3 minutes.

2 Place hot pasta in separate pan and mix with cheese. Simmer 2 minutes over low heat to melt cheese.

3 Pour hot cream over pasta and toss. Season with salt, pepper and paprika to taste. Simmer I minute before serving.

This recipe can be turned into an Alfredo Primavera by adding diced cooked vegetables to the sauce.

Ziti with Crabmeat and Lettuce
(4 servings)

3 tbsp	butter	45 mL
2	shallots, peeled and chopped	2
1	small head lettuce, washed, dried and thinly sliced	1
½ cup	dry white wine	125 mL
1½ cups	heavy cream	375 mL
1 tbsp	chopped fresh basil	15 mL
¾ lb	fresh crabmeat, cooked	350 g
1 lb	ziti, cooked al dente	450 g
	salt and pepper	
	cayenne pepper to taste	
	grated Parmesan cheese	

1 Heat butter in sauté pan over medium heat. Add shallots and cook 2 minutes. Add lettuce, season and cover. Continue cooking 3 minutes.

2 Pour in wine and cook 3 minutes over high heat.

3 Pour heavy cream into saucepan. Season well and cook 3 minutes over medium heat to thicken.

4 Pour cream over lettuce in pan, add basil and stir in crabmeat. Cook mixture 2 minutes over low heat.

5 Add hot pasta to sauce in pan. Season with salt and cayenne pepper. Toss and simmer 2 minutes.

6 Serve with Parmesan cheese.

Lasagne Ferrara
(6 servings)

3 tbsp	butter	45 mL
I	onion, peeled and chopped	I
2	carrots, pared and diced	2
I	celery stalk, diced	I
1/3 lb	prosciutto, diced	150 g
1/4 lb	ground veal	125 g
1/3 lb	lean ground beef	150 g
2	garlic cloves, peeled, crushed and chopped	2
I cup	dry white wine	250 mL
4	large tomatoes, peeled, seeded and chopped	4
2 tbsp	chopped fresh basil	30 mL
I lb	lasagne, cooked al dente	450 g
2 cups	White Sauce, heated (see p. 86)	500 mL
I cup	grated Parmesan cheese	250 mL
3/4 cup	grated mozzarella cheese	175 mL
	salt and pepper	

Preheat oven to 350°F (180°C).

1 Heat butter in large sauté pan over medium heat. Add onion, carrots and celery; cook 6 minutes.

2 Add prosciutto, mix and continue cooking 2 minutes. Add veal and beef; season well and brown 6 minutes.

3 Add garlic and wine. Cook 4 minutes. Add chopped tomatoes and basil. Season well and cook 8 min-utes to evaporate liquid from toma-toes. Correct seasoning.

4 Cover bottom of buttered lasagne baking dish with first layer of noodles. Spread half of ground meat mixture evenly over noodles.

5 Spoon layer of white sauce over ground meat. Add layer of Par-mesan and mozzarella.

6 Repeat layers, ending with grated cheeses. Bake 40 minutes in oven. Let stand 5 minutes before serving.

Cover bottom of buttered lasagne baking dish with first layer of noodles. Spread half of ground meat mixture evenly over noodles.

Spoon a layer of white sauce over ground meat.

Add a layer of Parmesan and mozzarella.

Repeat layers, ending with grated cheeses.

Rice Pilaf Pesto
(4 servings)

2 tbsp	butter	30 mL
2	shallots, peeled and chopped	2
1	celery stalk, finely diced	1
1 cup	long grain rice, rinsed and drained	250 mL
1 1/2 cups	chicken stock, heated	375 mL
1/3 cup	chopped fresh basil	75 mL
2	garlic cloves, peeled, crushed and chopped	2
1/4 cup	grated Pecorino cheese	50 mL
1/4 cup	grated Parmesan cheese	50 mL
1/2 cup	olive oil	125 mL
	salt and pepper	

Preheat oven to 350°F (180°C).

1 Heat butter in ovenproof casserole over medium heat. Add shallots and celery; cook 2 minutes.

2 Add rice, season and mix well. Continue cooking 1 minute. Pour in chicken stock, mix and bring to boil. Cover and bake 18 minutes in oven.

3 Meanwhile, place basil, garlic and grated cheeses in food processor. Season with pepper and blend. Add oil and blend until well incorporated.

4 Stir pesto into cooked rice and serve.

Basmati Rice with Spinach

(4 servings)

1 ½ cups	basmati rice	375 mL
3 cups	water	750 mL
1 ½ tsp	salt	7 mL
2 tbsp	olive oil	30 mL
2	bunches fresh spinach	2
1 ½	Spanish onions, peeled and sliced	1 ½
2	garlic cloves, peeled, crushed and chopped	2
	salt and pepper	

1 Rinse rice under cold water and drain.

2 Pour water into saucepan. Add salt and 1 tsp (5 mL) olive oil. Bring to boil. Add rice and stir. Cover and cook 30 to 35 minutes over low heat. If lid is not tight-fitting, more cooking time may be needed.

3 Meanwhile, prepare spinach. Remove stems from spinach. Wash leaves and cook in small amount of boiling water for 3 minutes or until wilted. Transfer spinach to sieve and squeeze out excess water by pressing with back of spoon. Shape spinach into ball and squeeze out all remaining water.

4 Heat remaining oil in frying pan over medium heat. Add onions and cook 15 minutes.

5 Add garlic and spinach. Season well and cook 4 minutes over high heat.

6 Incorporate spinach with cooked rice and serve.

White Rice with Vegetable Medley
(4 servings)

1 cup	long grain white rice	250 mL
3 tbsp	butter	45 mL
2	shallots, peeled and finely chopped	2
1/2 cup	dry white wine	125 mL
2 1/4 cups	light chicken stock, heated	550 mL
5	fresh asparagus stalks	5
1	red bell pepper, thinly sliced	1
1/4	zucchini, sliced in julienne	1/4
1/2 cup	grated Pecorino Sardo cheese	125 mL
	salt and pepper	

1 Rinse rice in cold water and drain.

2 Heat butter in saucepan over medium heat. Add shallots and cook 2 minutes over low heat. Add rice and mix well. Season and cook 2 minutes over medium heat.

3 Pour in wine, increase heat to high, and cook 2 minutes. Mix in chicken stock and correct seasoning. Cover and cook rice 20 minutes over low heat or until liquid is absorbed.

4 Just before serving rice, prepare vegetables. Pare asparagus stalks if necessary and trim stem ends. Cut stalks in 1-in (2.5-cm) lengths.

5 Blanch vegetables in small amount of salted, boiling water for 2 minutes.

6 Drain vegetables and serve over rice with cheese.

Baked Rice with Chicken Livers
(4 servings)

5 tbsp	butter	75 mL
I	onion, peeled and finely chopped	I
I cup	long grain rice, rinsed and drained	250 mL
I ½ cups	chicken stock, heated	375 mL
I	bay leaf	I
I tbsp	chopped fresh parsley	15 mL
I lb	chicken livers, cleaned and halved	450 g
2	shallots, peeled and finely chopped	2
2	garlic cloves, peeled, crushed and chopped	2
½ lb	fresh mushrooms, cleaned and halved	225 g
½ cup	dry white wine	125 mL
	salt and pepper	

Preheat oven to 350°F (180°C).

1 Heat 2 tbsp (30 mL) butter in ovenproof casserole over medium heat. Add onion and cook 2 minutes. Stir in rice and continue cooking 3 minutes.

2 Pour in chicken stock and season well. Add bay leaf and parsley; bring to boil. Cover and cook 18 to 20 minutes in oven.

3 Heat remaining butter in frying pan over medium heat. Add chicken livers, shallots and garlic; season well. Cook 5 minutes over high heat. Remove chicken livers from pan and set aside.

4 Add mushrooms to hot pan and continue cooking 5 minutes over high heat. Return chicken livers to pan and pour in wine. Cook 3 minutes over high heat. Remove bay leaf.

5 Pour mixture over rice, mix and serve.

Mexican Rice
(4 servings)

2 tbsp	olive oil	30 mL
1	onion, peeled and chopped	1
3	garlic cloves, peeled	3
1 cup	long grain rice, rinsed and drained	250 mL
1	red bell pepper, diced	1
2	large tomatoes, peeled, seeded and chopped	2
2 cups	beef stock, heated	500 mL
	salt and freshly ground pepper	
	generous pinch of saffron	
	crushed chilies to taste	

1 Heat oil in sauté pan over medium heat. Add onion and garlic; cook 4 minutes. Be careful not to let onion burn. Remove garlic cloves and set aside.

2 Add rice to hot pan and cook until browned. Stir frequently.

3 Force garlic cloves through garlic press; add to rice. Stir in remaining ingredients and correct seasoning.

4 Cover and cook rice 20 minutes over low heat. Add more stock if necessary. Serve with a broiled cut of meat.

Rice Creole with Chicken Wings
(4 servings)

WINGS:

30	chicken wings	30
I cup	soy sauce	250 mL
½ cup	brown sugar	125 mL
½ cup	butter	125 mL
3	blanched garlic cloves, puréed	3
I tsp	English mustard	5 mL
2 tbsp	Worcestershire sauce	30 mL
¾ cup	water	175 mL

1 Arrange chicken wings in single layer in large baking dish. Set aside.

2 Place remaining ingredients in saucepan. Cook 5 minutes over medium heat. Pour mixture over wings and marinate at least I hour in refrigerator.

3 Preheat oven to 350°F (180°C).

4 Remove wings from marinade and transfer to ovenproof tray. Bake 25 to 30 minutes in oven or adjust time according to size. Baste frequently with marinade during cooking.

RICE:

I ⅓ cups	water	325 mL
I tbsp	butter	15 mL
I tbsp	white vinegar	15 mL
I tbsp	sugar	15 mL
I cup	long grain white rice, rinsed	250 mL
	salt	

1 Place water, butter, vinegar, sugar and salt in saucepan. Add rice and bring to boil, stirring constantly.

2 Cover tightly and cook 25 to 30 minutes over very low heat. Let stand 5 minutes before serving with chicken wings.

Shrimp and Vegetables with Steamed Rice
(4 servings)

2 tbsp	olive oil	30 mL
1 lb	fresh shrimp, peeled and deveined	450 g
4	shallots, peeled and quartered	4
4	green onions, cut into sticks	4
1	yellow bell pepper, cubed	1
1	celery stalk, sliced	1
2	carrots, pared and thinly sliced	2
1	stalk bok choy, sliced	1
2	garlic cloves, peeled, crushed and chopped	2
2 tbsp	soy sauce	30 mL
1 ¼ cups	long grain white rice, rinsed and steamed	300 mL
	salt and freshly ground pepper	
	lemon juice	

1 Heat half of oil in frying pan over high heat. When very hot, add shrimp and cook 1 minute. Season well, turn shrimp over and continue cooking 1 minute. Remove shrimp from pan and set aside.

2 Wipe pan clean with paper towels. Add remaining oil to pan. When hot, add vegetables and garlic; season well. Cover and cook 2 minutes over high heat. Stir and continue cooking 1 minute.

3 Remove cover and cook 2 minutes. Add soy sauce, shrimp and lemon juice; season well.

4 Serve steamed rice in large platter. Top with shrimp and vegetable mixture.

Risotto with Parmesan
(4 to 6 servings)

1¾ cups	short grain white rice	425 mL
6 cups	very light chicken stock	1.5 L
2 tbsp	butter	30 mL
1	large shallot, peeled and chopped	1
1	garlic clove, peeled, crushed and chopped	1
½ cup	dry white wine	125 mL
1 cup	grated Parmesan cheese	250 mL
	salt and pepper	

1 Rinse rice under cold water and drain.

2 Bring chicken stock to boil in saucepan over medium heat. Reduce heat to maintain stock at a simmer.

3 Heat butter in separate saucepan over medium heat. Add shallot and garlic; cook 2 minutes.

4 Add rice and continue cooking 2 minutes. Pour in wine and cook 3 minutes. Season well.

5 Begin incorporating hot chicken stock to rice by adding 1 cup (250 mL) to saucepan, stirring constantly. Cook over medium-low heat. As the liquid evaporates, add more chicken stock, about ½ cup (125 mL) at a time. The trick to making a good risotto is to add the liquid a little at a time and to stir constantly. Total cooking time is about 25 minutes.

6 Two minutes before rice is cooked, stir in cheese.

Steamed Rice with Vegetables and Chicken
(4 servings)

8 cups	salted water	2 L
1¼ cups	long grain converted rice, rinsed	300 mL
2 tbsp	olive oil	30 mL
1	small whole chicken breast, skinned, boned and cut into strips	1
1 tbsp	chopped fresh ginger	15 mL
5	green onions, cut into sticks	5
1	small zucchini, cut into short sticks	1
1	red bell pepper, sliced	1
2 tbsp	soy sauce	30 mL
¼ cup	toasted cashew nuts	50 mL
	freshly ground pepper	

1 Pour water into large saucepan and bring to boil. Add rice and resume boil. Cook 10 minutes.

2 Drain rice into sieve. Place under cold running water. Position sieve over saucepan containing boiling water. Drape cloth over sieve and cover pan. Steam rice 15 minutes.

3 Meanwhile, heat oil in frying pan over high heat. Add chicken and season well. Cook strips, browning on all sides, about 5 minutes. Remove chicken from pan and set aside.

4 Add ginger and vegetables to hot pan. Cook 2 minutes. Return chicken to pan and stir in soy sauce and cashew nuts. Cook 1 minute and serve with steamed rice.

Baked Seafood Rice with Mayonnaise Sauce
(4 servings)

2 lb	littleneck clams, scrubbed	900 g
2 lb	mussels, bearded and scrubbed	900 g
2	shallots, peeled and chopped	2
1 tbsp	chopped fresh parsley	15 mL
¾ cup	dry white wine	175 mL
2 tbsp	butter	30 mL
1	onion, peeled and chopped	1
1¼ cups	long grain rice, rinsed and drained	300 mL
1½ cups	frozen green peas	375 mL
1	recipe Mayonnaise Sauce (see p. 86)	1
	salt and freshly ground pepper	

1 Place clams, mussels, shallots, parsley, wine and pepper in sauté pan. Cover and bring to boil. Cook over low heat until shells open, about 5 minutes. Stir once during cooking process.

2 Remove mussels and clams from pan, discarding any unopened shells. Set aside and keep warm. Pass cooking liquid through sieve lined with cheesecloth.

3 Preheat oven to 350°F (180°C).

4 Heat butter in ovenproof casserole over medium heat. Add onion and cook 3 minutes. Add rice and mix well. Continue cooking 2 minutes.

5 Pour in 2 cups (500 mL) of cooking liquid from seafood. If necessary, add water to fill measure. Season rice well and bring to boil. Cover and bake 18 minutes in oven.

6 Meanwhile, place peas in salted boiling water. Reduce heat and simmer until tender. Place under cold running water briefly, drain well and set aside.

7 Shell seafood and add to cooked rice. Add peas, mix and stir in mayonnaise sauce. Let rice stand 5 minutes before serving.

Rice Catalonia
(4 servings)

1 cup	long grain rice, rinsed and drained	250 mL
2¼ cups	light chicken stock	550 mL
2 lb	mussels, bearded and scrubbed	900 g
2	shallots, peeled and chopped	2
½ cup	dry white wine	125 mL
6 oz	chorizo sausage, sliced and cooked	175 g
1 cup	diced smoked Virginia ham	250 mL
2	tomatoes, peeled, seeded and diced	2
1	green bell pepper, diced	1
3 tbsp	olive oil	45 mL
2 tbsp	chopped fresh Italian parsley	30 mL
	salt and freshly ground pepper	
	juice of 1 lemon	

1 Place rice in boiling chicken stock. Cover and cook 20 minutes over low heat. Place under cold running water briefly, drain well and set aside.

2 Place mussels, shallots, wine and pepper in sauté pan. Cover and bring to boil. Cook mussels over low heat until shells open, about 5 minutes. Stir once during cooking.

3 Remove mussels from pan, discarding any unopened shells. Shell mussels and place in bowl.

4 Add rice, sausage, ham, tomatoes and green pepper. Season well and squeeze in lemon juice.

5 Add oil and parsley; mix very well. Season with pepper, mix and serve.

Mock Jambalaya
(4 to 6 servings)

1 tbsp	olive oil	15 mL
½ lb	chorizo sausage, sliced ¼ in (5 mm) thick	225 g
2	onions, peeled and chopped	2
1	green bell pepper, diced	1
1	red bell pepper, diced	1
2	garlic cloves, peeled, crushed and chopped	2
1	bay leaf	1
¼ tsp	thyme	1 mL
2	large tomatoes, peeled, seeded and diced	2
1 cup	long grain white rice	250 mL
2 cups	light chicken or fish stock, heated	500 mL
1 lb	cooked crabmeat	450 g
½ lb	cooked shrimp	225 g
	salt and pepper	
	few drops of Tabasco sauce	

1 Heat oil in large sauté pan over medium heat. Add sausage and cook 3 minutes. Add onions and continue cooking 3 minutes.

2 Add bell peppers, garlic, all seasonings and tomatoes. Cook 4 minutes over high heat.

3 Stir in rice and chicken stock. Mix well, cover and cook 16 minutes over low heat.

4 Add crabmeat and shrimp to rice. Cover and continue cooking 4 minutes. Remove bay leaf.

5 Serve with garlic bread.

Curried Scampi with Rice
(4 servings)

2 tbsp	olive oil	30 mL
3	shallots, peeled and chopped	3
1 tbsp	chopped fresh ginger	15 mL
1	jalapeño pepper, seeded and chopped	1
1 tbsp	curry powder	15 mL
1 lb	scampi, butterflied and deveined	450 g
1 ¼ cups	long grain white rice, rinsed and steamed	300 mL
	salt and freshly ground pepper	
	lemon juice	

1 Heat oil in frying pan over medium heat. Add shallots, ginger and jalapeño pepper. Cook 1 minute.

2 Sprinkle in curry powder; mix well. Add scampi and cook 2 minutes over high heat. Season well, turn scampi over and continue cooking 1 minute.

3 Add lemon juice and mix well. Cook 30 seconds and serve over steamed rice.

Indian Spice Rice
(6 servings)

2 tsp	whole black peppercorns	10 mL
2 tsp	cardamom seeds	10 mL
1 ½ tsp	whole cloves	7 mL
3 tbsp	peanut oil	45 mL
2 cups	long grain white rice, rinsed and drained	500 mL
4 cups	water	1 L
¼ cup	chopped cashew nuts	50 mL
¼ cup	grated coconut	50 mL
	salt	
	chopped fresh coriander	

Preheat oven to 250°F (120°C).

1 Place peppercorns, cardamom and cloves in baking dish. Bake 1 hour in oven. Place seasonings in mortar and grind finely.

2 Increase oven heat to 350°F (180°C).

3 Heat oil in ovenproof casserole over medium heat. Add rice and ground seasonings. Mix well and add salt. Cook 4 minutes over low heat or until rice starts to stick to bottom of casserole.

4 Pour in water and mix well. Bring to boil and cook 5 to 7 minutes.

5 Cover and continue cooking rice 15 minutes in oven.

6 Add remaining ingredients to rice and mix well. Continue cooking 3 to 4 minutes or until rice is tender.

White Sauce for Pasta Dishes

(4 to 6 servings)

4 tbsp	butter	60 mL
I	small onion, peeled and finely chopped	I
5 tbsp	flour	75 mL
4 cups	milk, heated	I L
	salt and white pepper	
	pinch of nutmeg	
	pinch of paprika	

1 Melt butter in saucepan over medium heat. Add onion and cook 3 minutes over low heat.

2 Add flour and mix well. Reduce heat and cook 1 minute, stirring constantly.

3 Pour in milk, mixing constantly with whisk. Season well and add nutmeg and paprika.

4 Cook sauce 10 minutes over low heat, stirring frequently. Pour sauce through sieve before using.

Mayonnaise Sauce

(4 servings)

½ cup	mayonnaise	125 mL
3 tbsp	lightly whipped cream	45 mL
2 tbsp	chopped fresh chives	30 mL
I	small celery stalk, finely chopped	I
I tbsp	chopped fresh parsley	15 mL
	salt and freshly ground pepper	

1 Place mayonnaise, whipped cream and chives in small bowl.

2 Add celery and parsley. Mix together and season generously; mix again.

3 Serve with Baked Seafood Rice (see p. 81).

Meat Sauce for Pasta

(6 servings)

8	tomatoes, cored	8
2 tbsp	olive oil	30 mL
1	large onion, peeled and finely chopped	1
4	garlic cloves, peeled, crushed and chopped	4
2	carrots, pared and diced	2
½ lb	lean ground beef	225 g
1 cup	dry red wine	250 mL
2 cups	beef stock, heated	500 mL
4	slices cooked ham, diced	4
5	slices prosciutto, diced	5
1 tsp	grated lemon zest	5 mL
2 tbsp	chopped fresh basil	30 mL
1 tsp	oregano	5 mL
2 tbsp	chopped fresh parsley	30 mL
	salt and pepper	

1 Plunge tomatoes in saucepan with boiling water. Remove tomatoes after 1 minute. When cool enough to handle, peel skins. Cut tomatoes in half horizontally and squeeze out seeds. Chop pulp and set aside.

2 Heat oil in large pot over medium heat. When hot, add onion, garlic, and carrots. Cook 8 minutes over medium heat.

3 Add ground beef and mix well. Season and continue cooking 6 minutes to brown meat. Reduce heat if necessary.

4 Stir in wine and beef stock. Add remaining ingredients and season well. Mix and cook sauce, partly covered, 1½ hours over low heat. Stir 2 to 3 times during cooking.

5 Sauce is ready when it is thick enough to hold its shape.

Bolognese Meat Sauce

(4 servings)

2 tbsp	butter	30 mL
2 oz	salt pork, diced	60 g
1	onion, peeled and chopped	1
1	carrot, pared and diced	1
1	celery stalk, diced	1
3 oz	lean ground beef	90 g
3 oz	lean ground pork	90 g
¼ lb	fresh mushrooms, cleaned and diced	125 g
¼ lb	prosciutto, diced	125 g
2 tbsp	tomato paste	30 mL
¾ cup	dry red wine	175 mL
¾ cup	beef stock, heated	175 mL
¼ tsp	oregano	1 mL
3 tbsp	heavy cream	45 mL
	salt and pepper	

1 Heat butter in sauté pan over medium heat. Add salt pork and cook 2 minutes.

2 Add onion, carrot and celery; season well. Continue cooking 4 minutes over medium heat.

3 Add ground meats. Season and cook another 4 minutes. Add mushrooms and cook 3 minutes.

4 Add remaining ingredients, except cream, and bring to boil. Cover and cook 30 minutes over low heat. Stir frequently during cooking.

5 Mix in cream and serve over hot pasta.

Meatless Pasta Sauce
(8 servings)

3 tbsp	olive oil	45 mL
2	garlic cloves, peeled	2
1	large onion, peeled and chopped	1
1/2	celery stalk, diced	1/2
1	carrot, pared and diced	1
2	garlic cloves, peeled, crushed and chopped	2
1 cup	dry red wine	250 mL
2	28 oz (796 mL) cans tomatoes, drained and chopped	2
5 1/2 oz	can tomato paste	156 mL
2 tbsp	chopped fresh basil	30 mL
1/2 tsp	oregano	2 mL
1/4 tsp	thyme	1 mL
	salt and pepper	
	pinch of sugar	

1 Heat oil in large pot over medium heat. When hot, add peeled whole garlic cloves. Cook until cloves brown, then remove garlic and discard.

2 Add onion, celery, carrot and chopped garlic to hot oil. Cook 8 minutes over very low heat.

3 Pour in wine and add remaining ingredients. Mix well, season and bring to boil. Mix well and cook, partly covered, 1 1/2 hours over low heat. Stir frequently during cooking.

4 Use this sauce for many pasta recipes. This sauce can be kept up to 4 days in the refrigerator.

Basic Tomato Purée
(6 servings)

12	tomatoes, cored and quartered	12
3	garlic cloves, peeled and crushed	3
1	large bay leaf	1
4	fresh basil leaves	4
½ tsp	oregano	2 mL
1	small sprig thyme	1
	pinch of sugar	
	salt and pepper	
	chopped fresh basil and parsley to taste	

1 Place all ingredients, except chopped basil and parsley, in large pot and mix well. Bring to boil. Reduce heat to low and cook ingredients 10 minutes.

2 Force mixture through sieve, discarding skins and seeds from tomatoes.

3 Place tomato purée in saucepan and season well. Add chopped fresh herbs and reduce volume by ½ over medium-low heat.

4 Use in a variety of pasta dishes.

Pesto Sauce with Spinach
(4 servings)

¾ cup	fresh spinach leaves	175 mL
¾ cup	fresh basil leaves	175 mL
1 cup	olive oil	250 mL
5	garlic cloves, peeled and crushed	5
¼ cup	pine nuts	50 mL
¾ cup	grated Parmesan cheese	175 mL
1 tbsp	chopped fresh parsley	15 mL
	salt and pepper	
	few drops hot pepper sauce (optional)	

1 Wash spinach and basil leaves well. Dry leaves and place in food processor.

2 Add oil, garlic, pine nuts and remaining ingredients. Blend until thoroughly combined.

3 Correct seasoning and add a few drops of hot pepper sauce, if desired.

4 Toss sauce with hot pasta.

Rouille Dressing

2	red bell peppers	2
1 tbsp	white breadcrumbs	15 mL
3	garlic cloves, peeled	3
5 to 6 tbsp	olive oil	75 to 90 mL

1 Slice bell peppers in half. Remove seeds and white membrane.

2 Place bell peppers, breadcrumbs and garlic in food processor; blend 10 seconds.

3 While machine is blending, pour oil in stream through hole in top to incorporate. Season well. Serve with Fusilli Salad (see p. 47).

Cheese Stuffing for Pasta

1	red bell pepper	1
½ cup	ground pine nuts	125 mL
¾ cup	ricotta cheese	175 mL
¾ cup	grated mozzarella cheese	175 mL
½ lb	grated Parmesan cheese	225 g
2	large eggs, beaten	2
1 tbsp	finely chopped lemon zest	15 mL
24	pitted green olives, chopped	24
¼ tsp	paprika	1 mL
	pinch of nutmeg	
	salt and pepper	

1 Cut bell pepper in half and remove seeds. Oil skin and place cut-side-down on cookie sheet; broil 6 minutes in oven. Remove from oven and let cool. Peel off skin and place pepper in food processor. Blend 30 seconds to purée.

2 Add remaining ingredients to food processor. Blend 1 minute. Season well and blend briefly to combine.

3 Refrigerate 1 hour before using. This stuffing is ideal for home-made ravioli, tortellini, cannelloni, etc.

Veal and Spinach Stuffing for Pasta

2	bunches fresh spinach	2
2 tbsp	olive oil	30 mL
1	onion, peeled and finely chopped	1
1	carrot, pared and diced	1
2	garlic cloves, peeled, crushed and chopped	2
1 1/2 lb	ground veal	700 g
1 cup	White Sauce, heated (see p. 86)	250 mL
2	egg yolks	2
3/4 cup	grated Parmesan cheese	175 mL
3 tbsp	white breadcrumbs	45 mL
1/2 tsp	paprika	2 mL
	salt and freshly ground pepper	

1 Remove stems from spinach. Wash leaves and blanch in small amount of boiling water for 2 minutes. Transfer spinach to sieve and squeeze out excess water by pressing leaves with back of spoon. Chop and set aside.

2 Heat oil in frying pan over medium heat. Add onion, carrot and garlic; cook 3 minutes over low heat.

3 Add veal and mix well. Cook 4 minutes over medium heat. Season well.

4 Stir in spinach and white sauce. Mix in egg yolks. Add remaining ingredients, mixing well to combine. Cook stuffing 3 minutes over low heat. Correct seasoning.

This stuffing can be kept up to 3 days in refrigerator. Use to stuff a variety of homemade pasta.

Chicken Stuffing for Pasta

2 cups	fresh basil, washed	500 mL
3 tbsp	olive oil	45 mL
2	shallots, peeled and chopped	2
2	garlic cloves, peeled, crushed and chopped	2
¾ lb	fresh mushrooms, cleaned and chopped	350 g
¾ lb	ground chicken	350 g
2	egg yolks	2
2 tbsp	white breadcrumbs	30 mL
2 tbsp	heavy cream	30 mL
¼ tsp	paprika	1 mL
	salt and pepper	

1 Blanch basil in small amount of boiling water for 2 minutes. Transfer basil to sieve and squeeze out excess water by pressing leaves with back of spoon. Chop and set aside.

2 Heat oil in frying pan over medium heat. Add shallots and garlic; cook 2 minutes over low heat. Add basil and mushrooms; season well. Continue cooking 4 minutes.

3 Add ground chicken, season and cook over medium heat until browned.

4 Transfer mixture to bowl. Add remaining ingredients and mix very well. Correct seasoning.

5 Refrigerate 1 hour before using as stuffing for homemade ravioli, tortellini, cannelloni, etc.

Seafood Stuffing for Cannelloni

(4 to 6 servings)

2	bunches fresh spinach	2
1 tbsp	olive oil	15 mL
1	onion, peeled and chopped	1
2	garlic cloves, peeled, crushed and chopped	2
1 lb	cooked shrimp, peeled, deveined and chopped	450 g
2 cups	White Sauce, heated (see p. 86)	500 mL
1	egg yolk	1
1 tbsp	white breadcrumbs	15 mL
¼ tsp	crushed chilies	1 mL
	salt and pepper	
	pinch of nutmeg	

1 Remove stems from spinach. Wash leaves and blanch in small amount of boiling water for 2 minutes. Transfer spinach to sieve and squeeze out excess water by pressing leaves with back of spoon. Chop and set aside.

2 Heat oil in frying pan over medium heat. Add onion and garlic; cook 2 minutes.

3 Add chopped spinach, season and mix. Continue cooking 4 minutes over medium heat.

4 Add shrimp and white sauce. Mix well and add egg yolk. Mix again and stir in remaining ingredients. Season well and cook 2 minutes over low heat.

5 Stuff cannelloni and prepare to bake. This stuffing can be kept up to 3 days in refrigerator.

Index

Baked Cannelloni	48	Pasta with Alfredo Sauce	68
Baked Cappelletti – Bohemian Style	51	Penne à la Diable	34
Baked Macaroni and Cheese with Meat Sauce	17	Penne in Mushroom Red Wine Sauce	38
Baked Rice with Chicken Livers	75	Penne with Hearts of Palm	63
Baked Seafood Rice with Mayonnaise Sauce	81	Penne with Sautéed Chicken in White Wine	25
Basic Tomato Purée	90	Pesto Sauce with Spinach	91
Basmati Rice with Spinach	73	Pork Tenderloin and Pasta Stir-Fry	35
Bolognese Meat Sauce	88	Quick Chicken Sauté over Pasta	31
Capelli d'Angelo Nouvelle	11	Quick Gnocchi Dough	10
Cheese Stuffing for Pasta	92	Quick Spaghetti and Clams in Red Sauce	58
Chicken Stuffing for Pasta	94	Ravioli in Gorgonzola Cream Sauce	61
Curried Scampi with Rice	84	Ravioli in Sun-Dried Tomato Sauce	57
Egg Noodles in Ground Lamb Sauce	64	Rice Catalonia	82
Farfalle with Mushrooms and Bacon	20	Rice Creole with Chicken Wings	77
Fettuccine and Fresh Watercress	27	Rice Pilaf Pesto	72
Fettuccine in Anchovy Tomato Sauce	39	Ricotta Spinach Lasagne	29
Fettuccine in Cream Sauce with Asparagus	14	Rigatoni Baked with Virginia Ham	43
Fettuccine Jambalaya	21	Rigatoni in Curry Sauce with Apples	40
Fettuccine Jardinière	67	Rigatoni with Salmon in White Sauce	50
Fettuccine Supreme	44	Risotto with Parmesan	79
Fettuccine with Smoked Salmon and Tomatoes	18	Rotelle Spinach Salad with Mustard Vinaigrette	12
Four-Cheese Macaroni	15	Rouille Dressing	91
Fruity Noodles with Pecorino Cream Sauce	55	Sauté of Shrimp with Pasta	46
Fusilli Salad with Rouille Dressing	47	Seafood Fettuccine in Smoky Sauce	19
Fusilli Tapenade	53	Seafood Linguine	13
Fusilli with Fresh Littleneck Clams	62	Seafood Pasta Salad	49
Hearty Eggplant Lasagne	28	Seafood Stuffing for Cannelloni	95
How to Cook Pasta	9	Shrimp and Vegetables with Steamed Rice	78
Indian Spice Rice	85	Spaetzle (German Noodles)	41
Insalata of Farfalle with Tuna	56	Spaghetti in Roasted Bell Pepper Sauce	32
Lasagne Ferrara	70-71	Spaghetti Tossed in Hot Olive Oil with Garlic	30
Linguine with Fresh Mussels in Tomato Sauce	45	Spaghetti with Chicken Livers	65
Linguine with Light Basil Sauce	60	Spaghetti with Pesto	33
Macaroni alla Caciocavallo	16	Spaghetti with Ratatouille Sauce	59
Macaroni and Celeriac Salad	22	Spaghetti with Shrimp and Mussels	26
Macaroni Niçoise	37	Steamed Rice with Vegetables and Chicken	80
Mayonnaise Sauce	86	Summer Harvest Pasta	52
Meat Sauce for Pasta	87	Toasted Walnut Pasta Salad	54
Meatless Pasta Sauce	89	Tortellini with Garlic Chicken Sauce	36
Mexican Rice	76	Veal and Spinach Stuffing for Pasta	93
Mock Jambalaya	83	White Rice with Vegetable Medley	74
Pasta Dough	8	White Sauce for Pasta Dishes	86
Pasta Pollo with Roasted Peppers	42	Zesty Linguine	24
Pasta Salad with Mixed Vegetables	23	Ziti with Crabmeat and Lettuce	69
		Ziti with Vegetables	66